Under Coogan's Bluff

Chapter and Cask

P.O. Box 113
Glenshaw, PA 15116

Under Coogan's Bluff

**A Fan's Recollections of the
New York Giants Under Terry and Ott**

by Fred Stein

Acknowledgment is made to Wide World
Photos for the cover picture and the 1937 team
photo of the New York Giants. All other
photos are credited to the National Baseball
Hall of Fame and Museum, Inc.

ISBN 0-940056-00-3
CIP and Library of Congress Data forthcoming

First Printing, April 1979

First 𝔊𝔥𝔞𝔭𝔱𝔢𝔯 𝔞𝔫𝔡 𝔊𝔞𝔰𝔨 Printing, July 1981

Printed in the United States by Automated Graphic Systems, Inc.

To my wife, who pulled the pieces together,
and to Cynthia, Danny, and Billy,
who love the game as I do.

Foreword

Suppose you had a dream it was afternoon at the Polo Grounds in the 1930's (and don't think that people from that time don't have them), you'd have the most beatific smile and your snore would be a purr. It was the happiest place in town. Finally you'd snap awake. No use, those days are gone forever.

But hold on. You can live them again as Fred Stein (address: Row 5, Polo Grounds bleachers any afternoon), in his *Under Coogan's Bluff,* lures you to dreamland. Before you know it, Travis Jackson is throwing out a runner, Mel Ott is kicking up his right leg, fans are sunning upstairs in left field, players are walking off to the clubhouse stairs in center field after the game, followed by the crowd . . . it all comes back, the horseshoe, Chinese home runs, left field wall.

Seniors hug the good old ball field memory in any era, anywhere—pennants, longest home runs, fights, all-time teams; who doesn't? It's as appealing universally as your family album. What's so wonderful about the Polo Grounds? You'll see. One hundred fifty-fifth Street and Eighth Avenue seems indelibly stamped in the hearts of those fortunate enough to have been there. Juniors are not apt to set this volume down either . . . if only to figure out why. The difference from today, that's what's so wonderful about the Polo Grounds.

Forty years from now will Fred Stein's grandson be so overcome with nostalgia that he will write a book about the warmth and sentiment of the 1970's and '80's, when nobody had any angle?

Off to dreamland with you.

Ken Smith
National Baseball Hall of Fame
Cooperstown, New York

Preface

These are the recollections of a one-time, impassioned New York Giant baseball fan which, I hope, will provide enjoyment and nostalgic recall to my erstwhile co-fanatics. Essentially I have covered the period from 1933, when as a small boy I discovered the Giants, through the 1940's when the U.S. Army discovered me.

I have written this book for several reasons. First, I was fascinated by the intermix of personalities of the players, fans, and writers of the era as well as the actual games and pennant races, and I wanted to set my personal impressions down in some systematic historical and anecdotal form.

In addition, I have read many books on sports but have yet to see one written by a *fan* for other fans, as opposed to books written by professional writers or principal characters.

Finally, although there have been excellent books by Frank Graham and Joseph Durso describing the John McGraw era, nothing has been written about the Giants in the years following 1932. This book chronicles the Bill Terry and Mel Ott regimes; I leave the ensuing years for another writer.

For the time being, though, I'll be completely satisfied if this book renews your recollection of a time when life was simpler, when 155th Street was the site of the Polo Grounds rather than a housing development, and when happiness was no further away than the next Giant victory.

Fred Stein
6333 Beryl Road
Alexandria, Virginia

Contents

1

The Polo Grounds, Media, and Fans

The Polo Grounds, built in the 1890's and torn down in the name of progress in 1963 to make way for a housing development, was something special. Like many of the older parks built in the early 1900's (actually the Polo Grounds was the only major league park built before 1900), it had a unique charm and atmosphere which the newer stadiums are not likely to match.

Situated in a hollow overlooked by a mini-cliff known as Coogan's Bluff, the old, rectangular-shaped park was located near 155th Street in Manhattan, just across the Harlem River from the Yankee Stadium. It was bounded on its home plate side by Coogan's Bluff and the "Speedway" (now the Harlem River Drive), a picturesque road running along the Harlem River from 155th Street to 200th Street in upper Manhattan. Outside its first base and right field stands was an enormous lot used extensively by local cricket teams. The third base and left field stands were bounded by subway train yards, and the street bordering the park's centerfield area was sun-sheltered by an IRT elevated station.

The green, double-decked horseshoe-shaped stands seated about 56,000. The unusual layout included high fences 257 feet down the right field line and 279 feet down the left field line and a center field which terminated 483 feet from the plate at the base of the clubhouse wall. Right and left field bleachers, fronted by large, green "batters' background" screens 460 feet from the plate, were separated by about 25 feet of open space extending from the screens back to the clubhouses. Each inner bleacher side had a flight of stairs leading to the separated clubhouses (the Giants on the right field side and their opponents on the left field side). The bullpens were in the outfield corners of the playing field. Owner Charles A. Stoneham's office, later used by his son Horace, was located

1

above the clubhouses in company with two ancient, iron loudspeakers and a large clock.

The Polo Grounds was ideal for hitters capable of pulling the ball directly down the line. However, the distances from the plate to the fences increased sharply from the foul lines out, and many long drives which were not hit close to the foul lines were converted into easy outs. The narrowness of the park also permitted outfielders to play relatively close to each other, thereby reducing the chances of hitting extra-base drives between the outfielders.

The outfield walls were probably the most difficult to play of any major league ball park and not only because of their sharp angles. The right field wall presented a solid stretch of concrete where most drives struck. Accordingly, a hard drive off the wall was likely to rebound back towards the infield. Balls hit not quite so hard most often caromed off towards center field, and softer drives, particularly those that just reached the wall, usually bounced off towards right center field or continued bouncing along the wall.

The left field wall was even more difficult to play. Compounding the problems encountered in playing the carom, the left field wall had a corrugated iron door on its gate which caused particularly unpredictable rebounds. Judgment of fly balls was complicated further because this was the sun field. In addition, the upper deck facing extended well out past the lower deck. This meant that in cases where fly balls just missed the upper deck there was a split second during which the fielder frequently lost sight of the ball.

Normally, distances from home plate are indicated by painted numerals on the wall which have no effect on outfield play. But not in the Polo Grounds. Because of the slanted view of the outfield walls from behind the plate, signs on the walls could not be read. Instead, markers were placed along the bottom of the walls to indicate distances from home plate. Made of tin or sheet steel and about 15 inches off the ground, they were set about two or three inches from the wall. When a drive struck a marker the rebound would behave unpredictably—either stopping dead or rolling along the base of the wall.

The outfield walls, as in all the older ball parks, were covered by advertising (GEM razor blades, Stahl-Meyer frankfurters, Botany clothes, etc.) until 1948. After that the walls were painted a restful green to conform with the rest of the park, which may not have pleased the outfielders who had used the letters in the advertisements as reference points in judging rebounds.

There was only one point outside the park from which any field action could be seen. This was an area high above Coogan's Bluff where a small portion of the field—the second base area and a small part of the outfield—was visible. An experienced viewer could have a good idea of

2

what was taking place on the field simply by watching this sector and listening to the changing crowd noises. This was before the day of the portable radio and, for that matter, before the Giant games were on radio.

Despite the great distance from the bleachers to the plate and the fact that many seats were obstructed by pillars, the Polo Grounds was a great park in which to see a ball game. I often recall my favorite seat in the bleachers (55 cents including tax) when I see a baseball game on TV. When the center field camera focuses on the plate, the view is similar to the familiar bleacher vantage point.

In an attempt to duplicate my old perspective in new surroundings, I took my two sons to a game at Robert F. Kennedy Stadium in Washington, D.C., some years ago when Washington had a "major league" team. We sat in the center field seats well above the scoreboard. I was disappointed and almost frightened by the difference. Nostalgia became the farthest thing from my mind. For one thing, the center field seats I knew at the Polo Grounds were at ground level in comparison with the RFK seats which are cloud-scrapingly high. And then there was an air of intimacy and belonging at the Polo Grounds in contrast to the cold, out-of-it feeling that assailed me as I tried to make out the batter. Maybe it was middle age, acrophobia, or maybe the Senators were just not my team. But it simply wasn't the same.

I also missed the manually operated scoreboard at the Polo Grounds. If you looked through binoculars, you could spot a face, a hand, or even a pair of eyes peering through the scoreboard openings as numerals were changed and the opening was uncovered for a few seconds. The new stadiums have electronically operated scoreboards, with no visible sign of a human presence.

Finally, there were no extraneous sounds or signs to bother us in those days. Enjoying the game was a personal thing and we could root vocally or quietly, as we desired. We were not forced to listen to almost continual, loud, ear-pounding organ music between innings and even between batters or pitches. There were no admonitions on the scoreboard to shout "Charge!" at a given signal. We were not reminded constantly of the attendance, as though this was some kind of personal challenge in which our participation was a matter of community pride. We were not informed endlessly about groups who had come all the way from Amelia, Virginia, or wherever, and who deserved our attention by the simple act of attendance. There were no pantyhose days or other promotional gimmicks. The menu at the Polo Grounds was strictly baseball, and that was the way we liked it.

The Giants left the Polo Grounds for San Francisco after the 1957 season in hot pursuit of Walter O'Malley's newly created Los Angeles Dodgers and, more important, California greenbacks. The Polo Grounds was not used again for major league baseball until 1962 when the infant,

3

spectacularly inept, New York Mets used it during the 1962 and 1963 seasons while waiting for the construction of Shea Stadium to be completed. Shortly after, the Polo Grounds was torn down to make way for a housing development, almost symbolically sharing the same fate as the Brooklyn Dodgers' Ebbets Field.

Roger Kahn expressed a poignant thought about Ebbets Field in *Sports Illustrated* in the summer of 1974 which could apply as well to the Polo Grounds with the substitution of names and dates. Kahn wrote:

> When the wreckers came in 1957, I felt no pangs. Walter O'Malley was a money man . . . . Let it go, let it go, like the past.
> Now through the years it haunts me. . . . I can see again a child's forgotten afternoon, when he walked with his father, through arcs of sunlight, and saw the bright flags, blue and green and white and red, the flapping flags that meant Ball Game Today. I wonder if a child can feel such stirrings walking toward the modular stadiums of the present. I wonder if children lack for having no neighborhood ball park; no preposterous right-field wall, or any Carl Furillo; no sense that this park represents their town, which is itself unique, as cities were before the planners came with steel and glass skyscrapers.

Like Roger Kahn and many others, I wonder too.

Before radio and TV, Giant fans were not completely dependent on newspaper reports. Ticker tape reports from the park continued well into the 1930's. Business offices in the lower Manhattan area, newspaper offices, and even bars would attract good-sized crowds during important regular season games. The ticker tape reports were received about 15 to 30 minutes after the action took place. Although ticker tape results most often would be shown inning by inning, they were frequently presented in more detailed, elaborate fashion.

Six-foot long signboards, representing miniature versions of the actual ball field, simulated game situations by a system of moving and blinking light bulbs. The flight of the ball would be depicted by a moving light, and blinking lights showed the position of baserunners. A large, lettered card was used to illustrate or describe plays not clearly shown by the light bulbs.

Many bars installed a ticker tape and encouraged the public to enter the premises and follow the game "hot off" the ticker. With beer at 10 cents a glass, barkeepers would offer "free lunch" consisting of sliced bread, tiny cuts of pickled herring, and delicatessen tidbits. All this and a "live" ball game for the price of a couple of beers!

The original Giant radio broadcasters in 1939 were Arch McDonald and Mel Allen. McDonald was an experienced, but unspectacular, import from the Washington Senators' radio team. Allen, of course, became famous later on as the "Voice of the Yankees" in their glory days in the 1940's and 1950's. Al Helfer, Ernie Harwell, Steve Ellis, Don Dunphy, Bill Slater, and Frankie Frisch were others who manned the Giants' radio

4

microphone in later years. Stan Lomax was one of the early radio sports reporters with a widely followed sports program every night on WOR. I also recall a 15-minute re-creation of the home team's games every evening at 7:15 narrated by Bert Lee and later by Marty Glickman.

The Giants began televising a small number of home games in 1947 over station WNBT, with Bob Stanton the first TV announcer. In 1950, Russ Hodges joined the Giants' radio-TV team, having teamed with Mel Allen for several years covering the Yankee games.

The Giants, along with the Yankees and the Dodgers, had the most extensive press coverage of all major league clubs. There were reporters from at least 10 major New York City papers traveling with the Giants. Newspaper coverage was especially important to the fans in those days because commercial TV was many years off and the New York area was one of the last in the major leagues to have radio play-by-play.

The two morning tabloid papers, the *Daily News* and the *Daily Mirror*, featured extensive pictorial coverage of games along with daily reportorial coverage. A few of the *News* reporters who covered the Giants were the outspoken Dick Young, Hy Turkin, Jack Mahon, Harry Forbes, Dick McCann and, in the early 1930's, the famed Paul Gallico. Sports editor Jimmy Powers devoted many of his upbeat, sprightly columns to the Giants. Ken Smith (for many years Director of Baseball's Hall of Fame) covered the Giants continuously for the *Mirror*. His efforts were complemented occasionally by Bob Considine and Charles Segar. Sports editor Dan Parker contributed many stories about the Giants, his columns given a special flavor by his frequent use of poetry and dialect.

The other two morning papers, the *New York Times* and the *Herald-Tribune*, catered to the more scholarly reader, and their baseball reporters' styles reflected this. John Drebinger of the *Times* traveled with the Giants for many years, switching assignments occasionally with James P. Dawson, who more often covered the Yankees, and Lou Effrat. Columnist John Kieran (who became even more widely known through his appearances on radio's "Information Please") wrote many excellent pieces on the Giants as did his successor, Arthur Daley. Some of the prominent Giant reporters for the *Herald-Tribune* included Richards Vidmer, Stanley Woodward, Red Smith, Harry E. Cross, Bob Cooke, and Arthur E. Patterson.

Witty Tom Meany traveled with the Giants and the Yankees alternately during the 1930's for the *World-Telegram* and later was sports editor for the short-lived evening tabloid, *PM*, in the early 1940's. The *World-Telegram* had several other outstanding reporters covering the Giants including Tom Cohane (later to become sports editor of *Look* magazine), Joe King, Pat McDonough, and Dan Daniel. Daniel's assignments were most often with the Yankees, although he covered the Giants extensively. His answers to baseball questions sent in by fans and published in his column "Daniel's Dope" were impressive, not only for their crisp authority but because of Daniel's unabashed subjectivity. The *Telegram's* sports editor, Joe Williams, discussed the Giants with an appropriate mixture of authority, skepticism, and biting wit.

Garry Schumacher (later to join the Giants' front office) covered the Giants with authority and affection for the *Journal-American.* Occasionally, the assignment was given to others, including Max Kase, Lester Rice, and Jack Singer. Feature columnist Bill Corum also wrote many excellent columns and was especially effective in his recollection of the earlier McGraw era.

The *Sun,* before it merged with the *World-Telegram,* had fine coverage of the Giants. Will Wedge, the regular Giant reporter, rotated assignments infrequently with James M. Kahn, Wilbur Wood, Edward T. Murphy, Frank C. True, and Herb Goren among others. Gifted Frank Graham's featured column was excellent and was particularly enhanced by his verbatim interviews with players which, Lou Effrat informed me, were written without benefit of notes of any kind. The *Post* had an able group covering the Giants which included Jerry Mitchell, Stanley Frank, Harold Burr, and Jack Miley. Jimmy Cannon's brilliant feature articles, many of them on the Giants, had a distinctive, Hemingway-like quality. Bert Gumpert covered the Giants for the *Bronx Home News.*

The most prominent of a first-rate group of sports photographers of the era was Izzy Kaplan of the *Mirror.* Izzy, a short, fat, East Side product, was a familiar figure at the Polo Grounds in the 1930's snapping the action with his "Big Bertha" camera. (This was the time before the long-distance, zoom lens, and photographers were permitted on the field to get close-action shots.) Kaplan's tendency to speak in malapropisms made him the prime subject of Dan Parker's dialect columns.

Willard Mullin of the *World-Telegram* was perhaps the best known of the cartoonists of the period. His most famous characters were the rag-clad Dodger fan and "St. Louis Swifty," representative of the speedy St. Louis Cardinals of the era. The *Daily News'* Leo O'Meara and the *Journal-American's* Burris Jenkins, Jr., were among the other important cartoonists on the New York sports scene.

In retrospect, the 1930's and 1940's may have been the last of the golden years for the baseball writer. At least this is the view of the veteran Dick Young of the *Daily News,* who covered the Giants during the 1940's. Young decried the changes since that era in a July 1974 issue of *The Sporting News.* He wrote:

> I can remember when . . . covering the baseball team was the creme de la creme, the choice assignment. It had status; it had style. . . . Young writers aimed for it. Old writers clung tenaciously to it. There was only one way a young writer got the job. The guy who had it died. And by then the young writer wasn't so young any more.

6

> Once he got it, the new man clung to it—for 10 years, 20 years, 30 years. You went on a trip with the ball club, and the same writers were there. . . . The players came and went. Managers were fired and hired. Even the club owners changed, but not the writers.
>
> Today, if a writer makes three straight trips with a baseball club, people say, you still here? Players look at him strangely, as though he's retarded or something. How come he hasn't moved on to something worthwhile?

Young went on to say that the baseball beat is avoided like the plague. He blames subhuman travel conditions. With the universal adoption of night ball, he says the writer is up constantly, writing early edition stories, then covering the game, then flying. Summing it up, Young concludes, "I'm not trying to say it's the toughest job in the world, but it's no longer the fun it was and it's no longer the best job on the paper. That's why baseball doesn't attract the best writers any longer."

Fans in different areas and cities tend to be equally knowledgeable about baseball (or any sport for that matter) given a similar exposure to the game. However, just as each of the older parks had its own individual physical characteristics and mystique, its fans also had their own distinctive approach and reaction to the game.

Brooklyn Dodger fans always struck me as extremely knowledgeable in the ways of major league baseball. Yet these fans often exhibited completely bizarre behavior both at and away from Ebbets Field. I refer to a Dodger fan whose contribution to American sports folklore consisted entirely of bellowing "Cookie, Cookie" (for Cookie Lavagetto) at the top of his lungs, while exploding balloons continuously, during the entire game. Or one Robert Joyce who became so enraged after a Dodger loss in 1938 that he shot to death one tormentor and seriously injured another. Or one Frank Germano who physically attacked Umpire George Magerkurth at Ebbets Field in 1939 after a contentious game with the Cincinnati Reds. Or Hilda (The Bell) Chester who rang a cowbell continuously at games to spur her heroes on while her more introspective bleacher neighbors cringed or took refuge in quieter sections of Ebbets Field. Attribute it to the long, daffy, frustrating history of the Dodgers from World War I until just before World War II—there is no question that Dodger fans took the game and their personal involvement in it very seriously.

Yankee fans were far less demonstrative and emotionally involved. My recollection of the typical Yankee fan of that era is of a relatively quiet citizen, watching the game with casual detachment, with complete confidence in a satisfactory outcome regardless of temporary setbacks. Given the awesome offenses powered by a Ruth, Gehrig, DiMaggio, or Mantle combined with consistently effective, if underrated, defense and pitching, the Yankee rooter's serenity was completely justified.

Giant fans were a different, more sophisticated, breed. Not for us were the emotional excesses or theatrics of the Dodger fan or the quiet calm of the Yankee adherents. Our elders had participated in McGraw's and Mathewson's victories before and after World War I and the Giants' championships in the 1920's. We, their lineal descendants, shared with quiet dignity in the Giants' hard-won titles in the 1930's and in the miseries of the team after those great years.

The Giants traditionally were the favorites of the Broadway and show business crowd. McGraw had been a close friend of many of the entertainers during his years as manager. One of the Giants' top lefthanders, Rube Marquard, had married Blossom Seeley, a vaudeville and musical comedy star. A Giant outfielder of the early 1900's, Mike Donlin married Mabel Hite, a well-known comedienne of the time.

During the 1930's and 1940's, Toots Shor's restaurant in midtown Manhattan was the Giants' unofficial headquarters for the show business and sporting crowd. Jack White's Club 21 was another favorite haunt. White, himself, was famous for his method of signalling Giant victories and defeats. A Giant win was indicated by a large sign at the club entrance giving the score with embellished details. Defeats called for a curt "No Game Today" message.

Comedians Olsen and Johnson gave Mel Ott one of his most embarassing moments during an intermission of their famous extravaganza, "Hellzapoppin." They turned the spotlight on the Giant outfielder and presented him with a softball autographed by the cast. Brooding Oscar Levant was a red-hot Giant fan whose encyclopedic knowledge of the game in general, and the Giants in particular, often surfaced when he appeared on the radio and TV show, "Information Please." Ethel Barrymore was a devoted Giant rooter. Her particular favorite was the Giants' graceful second baseman, Burgess Whitehead. Actress Tallulah Bankhead commented that Whitehead had the moves of a ballet dancer, a veritable Nijinsky masquerading as an infielder.

The effervescent Miss Bankhead was perhaps the most baseball-happy stage figure of the time. She discovered the Giants sometime in the late 1930's and immediately embraced them with characteristic all-out enthusiasm. She even took the blame for one of their unhappiest of home stands as she noted in a *Sunday New York Times* article in 1947:

> Back in the summer of 1939 I thought I had hoodooed the Giants. I'd seen them play a dozen games in a row, save for matinee days, and they were doing fine until I invited the entire club to see a performance of "The Little Foxes." After the performance I gave them a buffet supper in the promenade off the first balcony—canapes and caviar and some of the minor beverages. First Hubbell couldn't come because he was going to pitch the next day. Harry Danning didn't show up because he had a poisoned foot. Jurges had spit in an umpire's eye and had just escaped from Alcatraz. But Ott and Jo-Jo Moore and most of the rest of them came and bashfully said they enjoyed the play.
>
> And what happened after that? The Giants lost eight in a row. Sure that

I'd hexed them, I stayed away from the park. I even barred my maid from the Polo Grounds.

According to some Bankhead-watchers, her enthusiasm for the game far outstripped her knowledge of it. Mel Ott, who wore No. 4, was her favorite Giant. It was reported that her mind nearly cracked at the 1939 All-Star game when there seemed to be four Mel Otts playing. Her most frustrating experience reportedly came when she ventured over to Ebbets Field and spent the afternoon rooting for the Dodgers' Dolph Camilli, also No. 4. How was she to know that the Dodgers, and not the visiting Giants, would be wearing the white uniforms that afternoon? Tallulah hotly contested this story with the tart response, "I'm no kin of Abner Doubleday's, and I have no desire to have my ashes cast in a silver urn at Cooperstown, but I know a hawk from a handsaw. I can tell Ott from Camilli on a clear day, even if I am nearsighted and color-blind."

Comments and questions from the nearby Polo Grounds stands were easily detected by players. Ott told, for example, about an amusing exchange with one of his more intense rooters in the heat of a close game in 1942, his first year as manager. The fan leaned over the right field wall to ask Ott whether one of the Giant runs in a previous inning was earned or unearned. The preoccupied Ott answered the question with an arms-spread gesture indicating that he did not know. The fan, unsatisfied by his response, asked in wonderment, "What have you been doing here for 17 years, anyway?"

The Polo Grounds was alive with rooters whose common interest was the Giants' welfare but whose individual favorites varied. Many preferred to sit in the left field area to root for Jo-Jo Moore, whose trademarks were a great throwing arm and extreme competence as a leadoff man despite his habit of swinging at the first pitch (usually anathema in leading off).

Dick Bartell, Burgess Whitehead, Travis Jackson, and Blondy Ryan were among the most popular infielders I can remember. I recall one of my right field bleacher comrades who felt he had a special rapport with Bartell. He was forever shouting to Bartell, "Get two, Richie-boy" every time an opponent's runner was on first base with a double play in prospect. Every fly ball hit anywhere near Bartell's shortstop area, regardless of its difficulty, called for an encouraging bellow, "Can-of-corn!" (easy fly ball). Catchers Gus Mancuso and Harry Danning had their adherents as did the individual pitchers, particularly Carl Hubbell, Hal Schumacher, and Freddy Fitzsimmons.

Ott was the resident idol from the time he took over right field in the late 1920's, through his prime in the 1930's, and through his difficult years in the early 1940's as playing manager. He was the reigning king of "Ottville," an unincorporated enclave in the right field stands and bleachers. Ott's quiet brilliance helped sustain Giant fans during the team's slumps and especially in the barren years following the Giants' last pennant victory in 1937. Ott also was my particular hero, as much for his unassuming, pleasant demeanor as for his accomplishments at the plate and in the field.

My favorite colleague in the right field bleachers was a round, swarthy, older man named Louie whose deep knowledge of the game and seniority as a bleacherite made him master of all he surveyed. Louie (his last name never came up and is completely irrelevant anyhow) impressed us mightily. He was in the habit of coming to the park a full two hours before the start of the game and occupying himself by reading Shakespeare and other classics not normally considered pregame entertainment in a ballpark. Moreover, the players recognized him and acknowledged his presence on their frequent pregame strolls to and from the Giants' first base dugout and the clubhouse. All of the bleacher occupants expected to be ignored by the players when we shouted encouragement and criticism to them as they walked across the field. No surprise then that we were deeply impressed by the response Louie received—"Howdy" from bouncy, little Dick Bartell, an agreeing nod of the head from Harry Danning when Louie reminded him of a mental error in the previous game, or a smile of recognition from Ott. As a group we gloried in the players' recognition of Louie and his baseball acumen.

On the rare occasions when I abandoned my bleacher plank for a grandstand seat, I particularly enjoyed sitting in the sunny upper deck behind third base. The occupants of that area, composed largely of refugees from the racetrack and nightclub circuits, were there to bet, not to root. They were past masters at the art of hedging bets. Whenever they placed or accepted a bet on the final outcome of a game, they would try to at least break even if their team was losing after four or five innings. To balance a potential loss, they would canvass the spectators and offer higher odds against their original choice. In effect, they were betting against themselves. More often than not, they would cancel out their potential losses with such a reverse maneuver.

Betting on the final score was only one of their angles. They also wagered on what the batter would do this turn at bat, whether the next pitch would be a ball or a strike, which section the next foul ball would fall in, and so on. All this in the face of stern "No Betting Permitted" signs scattered prominently around the park. I imagine their instinctive reaction if a ballpark policeman had tried to enforce the edict would have been an instant wager as to whether or not a culprit would be caught or how much he might be fined by the judge.

The writers, broadcasters, and fans did not drive in winning runs, make spectacular catches, or strike out opposing batters in clutch situations. Yet, in a real sense, they were as integral a part of the Polo Grounds as the players, managers, and umpires, and I remember them with the same fondness and nostalgic recall as I do the players and the Polo Grounds itself.

10

2

Terry Succeeds McGraw

When John McGraw began his thirtieth year as manager of the Giants in 1932, most baseball men rated him the greatest manager the game had known—10 pennants, only two seasons out of the first division, and a profoundly important baseball strategist and developer of talent. Despite a series of respectable first division finishes, McGraw was a troubled man as the Giants opened their spring training camp at Los Angeles in March. The club had not won a pennant since 1924. For the last few years managing had become more and more of a strain on the high-strung little Irishman. He suffered from a number of physical ailments, and his normal irascibility had intensified and led him into uncontrolled outbursts at anyone—the fans, other baseball officials, and his own players.

The players had developed a deep resentment of McGraw's rigid, strained, almost neurotic leadership. They detested his unreasonable disciplinary methods, the constant signs from the bench which inhibited their play, and the violent tirades. Freddy Lindstrom, a star since coming up as an 18-year-old "boy wonder" in 1924, was the most outwardly rebellious Giant. He and McGraw had engaged in shouting matches on the Giant bench before the entire team. And Lindstrom, a blithe, free-spirited, experienced player, was particularly incensed at the never-ending signals from the bench.

Frank Graham in his classic *McGraw Of The Giants* told a story, whether apocryphal or true, that typified Lindstrom's frame of mind and that of most of the other Giants as well. The Giants were playing a spring training exhibition game in Oakland. As Graham described it:

> McGraw, instead of sitting on the bench, sunned himself in the center field bleachers. . . . Mrs. McGraw, seated in a box near the dugout, was uncertain whether John was going to stay for the full game, so at the end

11

of one inning she called to Lindstrom (who was playing center field) . . . to have him ask her husband what he intended to do. Lindstrom didn't hear her and one of the reporters, seated near by, yelled to him and, as he turned, indicated that Mrs. McGraw wanted to speak to him. He came over to the box and she said, in mock severity: "Freddy! Why don't you pay attention?"

His eyes widened.

"Good God!" he exclaimed. "Are you giving signals, too?"

The other players, not as outspoken as Lindstrom, inwardly rebelled at McGraw's dictatorial style. Still, as the club moved east to open the season, it was rated the team to beat despite two straight pennants by the St. Louis Cardinals.

The Giants opened the season with Bill Terry at first base, Hughie Critz at second, Johnny Vergez at third, and Travis Jackson at shortstop. Mel Ott was the right fielder with Lindstrom in center and rookie Len Koenecke in left. Frank (Shanty) Hogan and the veteran Bob O'Farrell were the catchers. The pitching staff included two established starters, lefthander Carl Hubbell and Freddy Fitzsimmons, young Hal Schumacher, and veterans Bill Walker, Jim Mooney, Herman Bell, Waite Hoyt, Sam Gibson, and Dolph Luque.

Despite McGraw's high hopes, the club started off poorly and stumbled through April and May. The pitching was weak, the team was not hitting, and Travis Jackson suffered from serious knee ailments that forced him to the bench. Eddie (Doc) Marshall replaced Jackson with little success. (One writer was unkind enough to note that Marshall reminded him of an Ancient Mariner because he "stoppeth one of three.") McGraw's raw nerves worsened under the strain of losing, and the players reacted by tightening up even more. They were afraid of missing one of McGraw's innumerable signs or of making a mistake in the field and having to brave the tough little manager's ire. The net result was a team that was playing well below its capability. No one was surprised when the Giants began the month of June in last place.

On June 3, the Giants' doubleheader with the Philadelphia Phils at the Polo Grounds was rained out. The *World-Telegram's* Tom Meany headed aimlessly for the Giant clubhouse in search of a story or interview with no idea that he was falling into the biggest exclusive a New York sportswriter had obtained in many years. As Meany neared the clubhouse steps, a hot dog vendor asked him, "Did you know McGraw is out and Bill Terry is the new manager?" Meany then ran into Giant coach Tom Clark, who confirmed the story, pointing to a note on the clubhouse bulletin board. Meany read the full statement which described McGraw's lengthy consideration of the need to turn over the job to someone else because of his declining health. McGraw wanted a man "who was thoroughly familiar with the methods and who has learned baseball under me." Apparently a close personal relationship with McGraw was not a requisite, because

Terry told sports broadcaster Red Barber years later that he (Terry) had not been on speaking terms with McGraw during the two years before his appointment.

McGraw also expressed the belief that he was turning a good team over to Terry. That prompted Meany to comment pointedly, "McGraw was right when he said he was turning a good team over to Terry. It's a good club all right but McGraw couldn't handle those fellows any more. A few years ago he would have made those guys produce or they would have been gone. But Mac isn't well and he knows it's best that he get out."

The secret was so well kept that Lindstrom was the only player who had known that McGraw was actively considering stepping down. Lindstrom complained angrily to his friends among the writers that the job had been promised to him. From that day on it was clear that the outspoken Lindstrom would not be with the Giants much after the 1932 season—if he lasted that long.

William Harold Terry was a broad-shouldered young man from Memphis, who had joined the club as a lefthand pitcher in 1922. Even then he had no illusions about the glamor of big league baseball and was interested only in bettering the salary he was receiving from an oil company in Memphis. He surprised McGraw with his blasé reaction when offered a contract by the Giants. McGraw was not used to such independence in a young minor leaguer, and he probably admired Terry's attitude although he was never heard to admit it.

Terry took over with the clear understanding that he was the boss and not merely a frontman for McGraw. Assured of this, he stepped in and began to plan the moves he considered necessary to revitalize the Giants. He told the writers that he would make whatever changes he could, but that the season was too far gone to make any significant personnel shifts. The players were pleased by his first move though. Terry fired the club trainer, who was considered by many of the players to be McGraw's "stool pidgeon." This move alone raised club morale considerably.

Even without any player changes Terry succeeded in raising the club from last place to a sixth-place tie with the Cardinals, who also had flopped badly. Perhaps much of his success was inevitable. The Giants clearly had too much innate talent to remain in last place and the easing of tensions after McGraw's departure was bound to improve the club's play. After 40 games under McGraw, the Giants had won 17 and lost 23, a .425 pace. For the remainder of the season the club won 55 and lost 59, an improved .482 clip.

In light of the team's improvement the Giants gave Terry a two-year player-manager contract in September. It called for an estimated $30,000 a year, one of the highest salaries for any player or manager in those depression-ridden times. But the real impact of Terry's leadership was not apparent until after the season. Recognizing the need for a competent catcher, Terry swung a major deal with the Cardinals, obtaining second-string catcher Gus Mancuso and rookie pitcher Ray Starr for pitchers Bill Walker and Jim Mooney, outfielder Ethan Allen, and catcher Bob O'Farrell. The stocky, swarthy Mancuso would prove to be everything Terry wanted—a good handler of pitchers, durable, intelligent, and a key member of the Giants for many years to come.

Lindstrom had to go despite his great ability and long-time friendship with Terry because of unconcealed disappointment at not getting the managerial slot. At the end of the season Terry traded him to the Pittsburgh Pirates for outfielder George (Kiddo) Davis and pitcher Glenn Spencer.

In other offseason transactions of significance, pitchers Waite Hoyt and Clarence Mitchell were released and catcher Shanty Hogan was sold to the Boston Braves. Hoyt, well past his prime, had been a New York Yankee standout some years earlier. Hogan's gargantuan eating habits and the subterfuges he employed to hide his excesses from McGraw had provided the writers with a wealth of amusing copy. "Unfortunately," Tom Meany once cracked, "although Hogan eats like Babe Ruth, he plays like Hogan."

Although considerable publicity had been given McGraw's curfew rules, bedchecks, elaborate signals from the bench, and other tactics, it was clear these measures had not improved either team performance or esprit de corps. In his less flamboyant way, Terry set out to develop a more businesslike, no-nonsense approach to the game, a style more in keeping with his own personality. Typically, he had no immediate comment about off-the-field activities during McGraw's final managerial years, but his first public statements in 1933 stressed his desire for stricter control of his players' extracurricular pursuits and, unlike the free-wheeling McGraw, a close-mouthed attitude on the part of his players toward the press. It was clear that a new era had begun at the Polo Grounds.

BILL TERRY

3

The 1933 Team

On paper, the Giant club which began spring training at Los Angeles was not a pennant contender. The consensus of players, managers, and sportswriters throughout the league was that the Giants were facing a long season with only four proven stars, a prayer, and a string of nameless faces in Giant uniforms. The stars were rightfielder Mel Ott, Terry himself at first base, and pitchers Carl Hubbell and Freddy Fitzsimmons. The prayer was that gimpy-kneed shortstop Travis Jackson, out of action for much of 1932, could regain his old agility and play regularly. The nameless faces were legion.

Ott, beginning his eighth full year with the club at the age of 24, was one of the premier pluggers and outfielders in the game. A stocky, little left-hand swinger from the New Orleans suburb of Gretna, his distinctive batting style resembled that of the great Japanese League home run king, Sadaharu Oh (who claims he did not emulate Ott). As the pitcher prepared to throw the ball, Ott would lift his right leg high off the ground and raise and lower his bat vertically. Then, just before the pitch was released, his bat would become still, his head motionless, and he would place his right foot back on the ground shifting his weight from his rear foot to his front foot. The resulting forward momentum, combined with a quick wristsnap of the bat, gave him the ability to pull the ball sharply to right field for a surprising distance considering his relatively small stature. It also made him a particularly fearsome figure at the Polo Grounds with its short right field line.

At first base, Terry was one of the ranking stars of the day, a straighta-way line drive hitter who consistently hit for high average (the last National Leaguer to top .400 with a .401 average in 1930) and with power. Memphis Bill also was one of the best fielding first basemen ever to play the game. Moreover, he did not seem to permit his managerial duties to affect his playing.

Hubbell had pitched well since his first season with the team in 1928. The slender, frail-looking, lefthander possessed an adequate fast ball, a good curve, and marvelous control to accompany his famous screwball. The "scroogie" was simply a reverse curve which broke away from right-handed batters when thrown by the lefthanded Hubbell. Years of throwing the pitch with an outward reverse thrust of the elbow and wrist had caused King Carl's left palm and elbow to face out as his arm hung down at his side. The Meeker, Oklahoma, native was highly respected for his artful style and quiet concentration, his imperturbability in the pinch, and his ability to win the big game.

Fitzsimmons, a stout and stouthearted knuckleballer, was an off-season chicken farmer in Arcadia, California. He had an unusual "turntable" pitching style, whirling with his back to the plate before wheeling back around to deliver the pitch. Despite his bulky frame, "Fat Freddy" was an excellent fielder and was noted for his fiercely competitive approach to the game.

Travis (Stonewall) Jackson, from Waldo, Arkansas, had been the Giants' regular shortstop since the 1923 season before knee injuries limited his play in 1932. A steady hitter and fielder with a rifle arm, he was one of the most accomplished bunters in the league and was a great Polo Grounds favorite.

There were several other experienced players in camp. Roundfaced Sam Leslie was a good-hit, mediocre-field first baseman. Second baseman Hughie Critz, the pride of Greenwood, Mississippi, had been around for several years and was still considered a good fielder. Third baseman Johnny Vergez was a steady third baseman who had been hampered by injuries. George (Kiddo) Davis was a good outfielder but only a fair hitter. Outfielder Jo-Jo Moore, a gaunt, hollow-cheeked youngster from Texas with a great arm, had played for the club in 1931 and 1932. Gus Mancuso, obtained from the Cardinals in the big winter trade, was slated to be the first-string catcher.

The Giants had experienced pitchers as well. Terry was particularly high on Hal Schumacher, a slender, sinker-ball throwing righthander from Dolgeville, New York, by way of St. Lawrence University. A grim competitor with a hard-throwing, arm-wrenching motion, Prince Hal had pitched for the team in 1931 and 1932. Other pitchers included Ray Starr, obtained from the Cardinals along with Mancuso; Glenn Spencer, an ex-Pirate; LeRoy (Tarzan) Parmelee, whose nickname derived from his wildness; lefthander Al Smith; Herman Bell, a seasoned reliever; and Adolfo Luque, a wily 43-year-old Cuban relief pitcher whose National League career dated back to 1919 when he pitched for the Reds.

There were a number of promising youngsters in camp. The infielders included Smokey Joe Martin, a California product recruited by oldtime

18

Giant star Fred Snodgrass; Blondy Ryan, a spirited Holy Cross graduate; and Byrnie James. Rookie outfielders included Hank Leiber, a husky blond youngster from Arizona who had been brought to McGraw by ex-Giant pitcher Art Nehf; Homer Peel, up from the Texas League; and speedy Len Koenecke. Catcher Paul Richards, a Waxahachie, Texas, native later to gain wider fame as a field manager and general manager, was Mancuso's backup man.

The exhibition season began in unprepossessing fashion. It became apparent very soon that Travis Jackson's ailing knees had not recovered sufficiently to permit him to play regularly at shortstop. A disappointed Terry reluctantly installed the untried Blondy Ryan at shortstop.

Even the elements seemed to foreshadow a difficult year for the Giants. On March 11 during an exhibition game against the Chicago Cubs at Wrigley Field in Los Angeles, a major earthquake struck. While the ground trembled and the steel stands swayed, the terrified players huddled around second base. The following day, as the earth tremors continued to shake buildings, Terry announced tentative plans to move the club to Phoenix, Arizona, to complete spring training if the tremors continued another day. However, the upheavals subsided and the club completed its stay in Los Angeles before breaking camp and beginning its long exhibition game trek eastward.

Terry continued to experiment with different lineups. Always the realist, he recognized that the Giants' offense would depend primarily upon his and Ott's long-ball hitting and on the team's ability to come up with key hits. The players and managers had predicted a low-scoring year after playing a few exhibition games with the dead ball which would be used during the regular season. Terry sought to develop the team's defense, and the big questions here were how well Ryan would fill in for Jackson at shortstop and how much the veteran Critz had slowed down at second base. Finally, there was the pitching staff. Hubbell and Fitzsimmons were established stars, but would Schumacher fulfill his promise and Parmelee control his wildness?

One casualty of the barnstorming tour east was Coach Billy Southworth, who had suffered a minor knee injury during an exhibition game in El Paso. Typical of the bland reporting style of the day, the *New York Times* account stated simply that Southworth's injury would force him to return to his home "for an indefinite period" and that he would be replaced by ex-Giant catcher Frank (Pancho) Snyder. There were rumors that Southworth's quick replacement was the result of a violent disagreement with Terry, his old comrade-in-arms in the McGraw era during the 1920's. Memphis Bill turned up the next day with an unexplained black eye, which the *World-Telegram's* Tom Meany subsequently attributed to Southworth. The story, which would have been headline news in today's sensationalistic reporting, stuck despite denials by both Southworth and Terry.

19

As the Giants completed their exhibition game schedule and prepared to begin the regular compaign, their stock as pennant contenders remained low. The Associated Press annual sportswriters poll found 42 favoring the Pirates for first place, 21 picking the Cubs, 8 selecting the Cardinals, 8 picking the Phillies, and one each voting for the Dodgers and Boston. Overall, the Giants were ranked sixth, with only 18 intrepid prognosticators picking them for the first division—4 votes for third place and 14 for fourth place. With this unpromising outlook, the Terrymen faced the regular season.

The Giants were scheduled to open the season on April 13. Bad weather, sandwiched around a 1-to-1 tie with the Dodgers, postponed a decision until a week later when they beat the Phillies 3 to 2 on the solid pitching of Fitzsimmons combined with a game-saving relief effort by Hubbell. They plodded along steadily only to lose Terry with a broken wrist near the end of the month. However, the team continued to win as Sam Leslie filled in adequately for Memphis Bill. But the big story was Hubbell's pitching (26 consecutive scoreless innings), which earned him the nickname "Meal Ticket" from the writers and fans.

It soon became apparent that the Pirates, Braves, Cubs, and Cardinals would be the Giants' important competitors. The Pirates under manager George Gibson had powerful hitting but weak pitching. Manager Bill McKechnie's Braves were a weaker team, but they had three solid starters in Ben Cantwell, lefthander Ed Brandt, and Fred Frankhouse. Ex-Giant Shanty Hogan, still fighting his twin enemies—a knife and a fork—was the catcher.

The Cubs were a potent club with established regulars such as manager-first baseman Charlie Grimm, Bill Herman, Billy Jurges, Gabby Hartnett, and Frank Demaree and a pitching staff which included Guy Bush, Charley Root, and Lon Warneke. The Cardinals, led by ex-catcher Gabby Street, were an aggressive, up-and-coming team sparked by Frankie Frisch, Leo Durocher, Dizzy Dean, and Joe Medwick.

By Memorial Day the Giants had won 21 games and lost 16, nothing sensational but enough to position them in third place, 2-1/2 games behind the Pirates and three games in back of the Cardinals. Finally jelling, the Giants began to win a series of low-scoring games. Hubbell, Fitzsimmons, Schumacher, and Parmelee rotated starting assignments, and Luque, Bell, Starr, and the all-purpose Hubbell excelled in relief. Gus Mancuso proved a steadying influence behind the plate. The veteran Critz and youthful Blondy Ryan worked well together around second base, and Johnny Vergez fielded competently at third base and contributed several key hits. In the outfield Ott led the attack as expected, Jo-Jo Moore established himself solidly in left field, and George Davis handled center field adequately. Terry returned to the lineup in early June, and the Giants took over the lead on June 10 when Fitzsimmons defeated the Phillies.

On June 15, satisfied that his wrist had recovered satisfactorily, Terry traded Sam Leslie to the Dodgers for lefthander Watson Clark and outfielder Frank (Lefty) O'Doul. The trade was hailed by Giant fans as pennant insurance because Hubbell was the only lefthand pitcher on the staff and O'Doul, while showing some signs of wear and tear, had been the league batting champion in 1932.

One of the season's high points came on July 2 when the Giants won a memorable double-header from the Cardinals at the Polo Grounds. Hubbell pitched an incredible 18 scoreless innings to win the opening game 1 to 0, after Tex Carleton had pitched 16 brilliant scoreless innings for the Cards and had been relieved by Jesse Haines. Hubbell pitched perfect ball in 12 of the innings, allowing only six hits with no more than one coming in any inning. He struck out 12 batters and walked none. A single by Hughie Critz off Jesse Haines drove in the game's only run in the eighteenth inning. In the second game Parmelee, pitching in semi-darkness and a steady drizzle, shut out the Cardinals, again by a 1 to 0 score. The Giants' run came on a homer by third baseman Johnny Vergez. The one sobering note was a leg injury to Blondy Ryan, a spike wound requiring 13 stitches. Ryan was replaced by Travis Jackson.

Despite a double-header loss to the Braves on July 4, the Giants rested during the break for the first All-Star game with a five-game lead over the second-place Cardinals and a seven-game lead over the Pirates. Increased respect for the Giants was reflected in published gambling prices in which the Giants were quoted at 6 to 5 to win the pennant compared with the prohibitive choice they had been back in April.

After a loss to Dizzy Dean on July 11, the club's seventh in a row, the Giants received an unabashedly confident telegram from the injured Ryan. It read: "They cannot beat us. Am en route." That telegram remained posted on the bulletin board in the Giants' clubhouse and was to become the team watchword for the remainder of the season. On July 13, with a football shinguard protecting his damaged leg, Ryan replaced the faltering Travis Jackson and the Giants' fortunes again were on the upswing.

Hubbell continued his marvelous pitching, setting a record of 45 consecutive scoreless innings on August 1. He lost the game to the Braves, however, and the Giants slipped back to a 2-1/2-game lead over the second-place Pirates. With another concerted effort in August, the Giants fought their way back to a 7-1/2-game lead by Labor Day. The Pirates were in second place, followed by the Cubs and the Braves. The Cardinals, who had dropped to fifth place, had changed managers in August, replacing Gabby Street with Frankie Frisch.

There was another electrifying double-header against the Cardinals on August 27 at the Polo Grounds. The Cardinals won the first game 7 to 1 as Dizzy Dean defeated Schumacher. The second game was called because of darkness after eight innings following a tumultuous scene precipitated by the usually calm Terry. In the top of the eighth inning the Giants were leading 4 to 1, but the Cardinals threatened. With two men on, Frisch then sent a high, bouncing "Baltimore chop" to Terry, who grabbed the ball and dashed for first base, arriving there almost simultaneously with the headlong-diving Frisch. Umpire Ted McGrew called Frisch safe, and the lid blew off.

White with rage, Terry charged McGrew, who very emphatically waved the Giant manager off the premises with the traditional jerk of the thumb. Uncharacteristically, Terry responded by firing his cap and glove to the ground and kicking both vigorously. In the meantime, fans in the upper tier took a hand in the affair and soon pop bottles began raining down on the field. When order was finally restored after a riotous 15 minutes, McGrew caused even greater consternation by ordering peacemakers Mel Ott and Coach Tom Clarke off the field but permitting the infuriated Terry to remain in the game. After the game, Ott reported the following dialogue. McGrew: "Terry, you're out of here!" Terry: "You can't throw me out, I'm the manager and the only first baseman." McGrew, turning to Ott and Clarke who were trying to placate the raging Terry, then boomed: "OK, then you guys are out!"

In retrospect, the hectic scene was notable because Terry's violent outburst convinced Giant fans that he was something more than a robot—a fellow just putting in an afternoon. He was fighting to win and was wild when he thought an umpire's decision might steal away a Giant victory. As John Kieran wrote, "A tie was the best the team could get in the double-header, but the club won a real victory when the fans stood up and roared approval of Memphis Bill's explosion. They never knew that he cared. He lost the decision, but he won his spurs. The Old Guard among the Giant rooters has fallen in behind him."

Opening in Boston on their closing road drive to the pennant, the Giants dropped the first game and with that also lost third baseman Johnny Vergez for the season with appendicitis. Terry called on Hubbell the next day. With Travis Jackson replacing Vergez, the "Meal Ticket" turned in one of his masterpieces to win 2 to 0 in ten innings. Reformed baseball writer Heywood Broun, looking on from the press box, marveled at Hubbell's control as the great lefthander pitched his tenth shutout of the season. Hubbell not only did not walk a batter but never was behind a hitter at any time in the ten innings, or even went to a three and two count in the game. "Such control in a lefthander is incredible," wrote Broun. "There must be a skeleton in Hubbell's closet somewhere, perhaps a righthanded maternal grandmother."

Taking the next three games from the Braves, the Giants moved on to Pittsburgh. Although Hubbell was trounced by Larry French in the first game, the Giants managed to hold off the Pirates by splitting the next four.

Then came Chicago and the final threat. The Giants started this series by losing the first two games. But they came back to win the next four and knock the Cubs out of the race. The pennant was clinched in St. Louis on September 19 when the Pirates lost to the Phillies. Simultaneous with the announcement of the Pirate score, Ott, who had hit consistently in the pinch all year despite sub-par hitting statistics, blasted his twenty-third homer over the Sportsmans Park right field pavilion.

The exuberant Terry called the pennant victory his greatest thrill in 18 years in the game, especially in view of the club's low rating at the start of the season. Terry's satisfaction was fueled also by the assortment of criticism he had received around the league. In Boston he had been described as being "too aloof." In Chicago—and he carried the clipping around with him in his wallet—a writer had referred to him "as the most unpopular manager ever to win a pennant because of his surly disposition." In Pittsburgh they thought he lacked "color." Regardless, the Giants had won the pennant, winding up five games ahead of the Pirates, 6-1/2 in front of the Cubs, and nine games ahead of the Braves.

Noteworthy seasonal individual performances were turned in by Hubbell, Schumacher, Ott, and Terry. Hubbell led the league with 23 wins, 10 shutouts, and an astounding 1.66 earned-run-average. He was second to Dizzy Dean in strikeouts. Schumacher ranked in the top five in wins, earned-run-average, and shutouts. Ott was third in home runs and runs-batted-in, and Terry had the fourth highest batting average.

New York roared a boisterous welcome to the Giants as their special train arrived at Grand Central Station from St. Louis. A crowd of more than 10,000 headed by two brass bands put on a spontaneous demonstration that scarcely seemed possible in a city supposedly already surfeited with baseball pennants.

The Giants' official welcome took place the following morning at City Hall. Mayor O'Brien welcomed the team on behalf of the city, and brief congratulatory speeches followed from John McGraw and League President Heydler. Terry thanked the welcoming crowd and, despite his general dislike for all forms of ostentation, asked the crowd, "Do you want to meet the boys?" Following the predictably deafening response, Terry had each player step forward to take a bow.

Back at his desk in the Polo Grounds clubhouse, Terry waded through a pile of congratulatory mail and telegrams from all sections of the country. He got a big chuckle every time one of these began: "As one of the few who picked you to win. . . ." Later in the day came the news that the Washington Senators had clinched the American League pennant, and Terry began planning for the upcoming World Series.

The picture on the facing page was taken at the Polo Grounds during the second game of the 1933 World Series which pitted the Giants against the Washington Senators. In the second inning, with none out and no score, Travis Jackson prepares to sacrifice Mel Ott to third and George Davis to second. The Giants' conservative style—playing for one run as early as the second inning of a scoreless game—is unusual today, but was a successful strategy in that low-scoring year.

The empty seats reflect the severity of the Depression. Even at a World Series game, 20,000 of 51,000 grandstand and box seats ($1.10 admission and up) are empty, while all of the 4,600 bleacher seats (55 cents admission) are occupied.

The picture also shows the unusual configuration of the Polo Grounds. Note the short, 279-foot left field line with the stands extending sharply away from the plate to the visiting team's bullpen in front of the CANADA DRY sign. The Eddie Grant Memorial between the clubhouses in dead center was 483 feet from home plate. The banner-covered facing of the left field upper stands extended out well beyond the lower stands, adding suspense to apparently catchable drives to left field. In 1933 there were no field lights—the Polo Grounds was not equipped for night baseball until 1940.

The circle to the left of the BVD sign indicates the location of the author's customary vantage point.

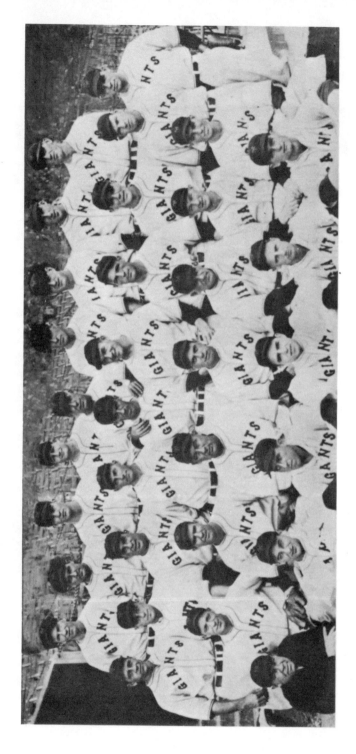

NEW YORK GIANTS—1933 WORLD CHAMPIONS

Back row: Bill Clark, Homer Peel, Jack Salveson, Bill Shores, Dolph Luque, Lefty O'Doul, Herman Bell, Harry Danning, Joe Moore; **third row:** Gus Mancuso, Johnny Vergez, Freddy Fitzsimmons, George Davis, Carl Hubbell, Blondy Ryan, Hal Schumacher, Joe Malay, Mel Ott, LeRoy Parmalee; **second row:** Hughie Critz, Travis Jackson, Frank Snyder (coach), Bill Terry (manager), Tom Clarke (coach), Chuck Dressen, Byrnie James; **front row:** Willie Schaeffer (trainer), Phil Weintraub, Al Smith, Tom Troy (mascot); Glenn Spencer, Paul Richards.

4

World Champions

The Washington Senators had won the American League pennant with relative ease, finishing seven games ahead of the heavily favored Yankees. Managed by their 26-year-old shortstop, Joe Cronin, the Senators were a solid ball club with a stronger attack than the Giants, a sound defense, and an accomplished pitching staff.

Smooth-fielding Joe Kuhel was at first base. Buddy Myer, a fine all-around player, was at second. Cronin at short was a better-than-average fielder and an exceptional hitter. Ossie Bluege, a defensive wizard, was at third. Heinie Manush, a lusty, high-average hitter was in left field. Center fielder Fred Schulte was a steady if unsensational performer. Leon (Goose) Goslin in right had been one of the American League's hardest hitters since joining the Senators 12 years before. Workmanlike Luke Sewell was the catcher. And the pitching staff, led by 20-game winners Alvin (General) Crowder and southpaw Earl Whitehill, also included starters Wally Stewart, Monte Weaver, Jack Russell, and relief pitcher Al Thomas. Because of their superior strength, on paper at least, the Senators were rated 10 to 7 favorites to win the Series.

A crowd of 46,672 jammed the spruced-up, banner-bedecked Polo Grounds for the first game. The early birds were out in full force, many appearing at the chilly bleacher entrances by midnight, long hours before squads of police arrived to maintain order. When tickets for the 4,600 bleacher seats went on sale at 10 a.m., about 12,000 fans stood in line, a remarkable tribute to the Giants' appeal in that Depression year. The tickets were snapped up in an hour, and thousands of would-be bleacher onlookers returned home in disappointment to listen to the game on radio.

The big attraction before the game was the standard comic routine of Al Schacht and Nick Altrock, baseball's foremost clowns of that era. The crowd rocked with laughter at their zany skits and antics—a hilarious tennis match featuring two incredibly inept but acrobatic players, a pepper game with skillful sleight-of-hand tricks with a bat and a ball, the inevitable game of catch with eggs that splattered the two deadpan participants, and the well-timed pratfalls and uncanny imitations of the players down to the last mannerism.

Tension began to build in the stands as the teams completed their warm-ups. The infield was rolled smooth as the pitchers came out to warm up. Hubbell, as expected, was the Giant starter. Cronin pulled a surprise by sending out lefthander Wally Stewart in an attempt to muffle Terry and Ott, the two Giant lefthand power hitters.

The Giants opened with a rush in the first inning as Hubbell struck out the side—Myer, Goslin, and Manush. All three were highly respected hitters, but no American League pitcher could throw a screwball comparable to Hubbell's.

Just as Hubbell dominated the top of the first inning, Ott took over the bottom half. Jo-Jo Moore led off with a sharp grounder that Myer bobbled for the first of his three errors on the day. Stewart got rid of Critz and Terry but he still had Ott to face. Master Melvin swung lustily at the second pitch and sent it on a low line into the right field seats about 400 feet away to move the Giants into a 2 to 0 lead.

In the third inning the Giants scored two more runs on hits by Critz, Terry, and Ott and a ground ball by Travis Jackson. That ended the Giant scoring for the day although Ott went on to a "4 for 4" binge with two more hard singles, the second almost removing Jack Russell's pitching arm as the drive whistled through the box.

The first seven innings were vintage Hubbell as the Senators scored only once on some uncertain play by the Giant infield. The Senators threatened in the eighth but were held scoreless as Goslin ended the inning with a scorching liner directly to Terry. Hubbell took a 4 to 1 lead into the ninth but ran into trouble as Washington loaded the bases with none out.

The Giants huddled at the mound. A worried Terry looked down to the Giant bullpen as Dolph Luque furiously pumped throws into Paul Richard's mitt. But Terry decided to stay with his meal ticket. Hub looked around calmly at the loaded bases, then went to work. He induced Kuhel to bounce out to Ryan as Manush scored to reduce the Giant lead to 4 to 2 with the tying runs at second and third. With the apprehensive home crowd roaring on every pitch Hubbell went to a 3 and 2 count before striking out Bluege with a crisp screwball. Luke Sewell worked Hubbell to a 2 and 2 count before topping a slow bounder down the third base line. Jackson hobbled in for the ball and threw a bullet to Terry to end the game. Giant fans let out a deafening roar as Terry trotted to the clubhouse with his arm around Hubbell's shoulders.

In the second game it was Crowder against Schumacher, with the Giants winning 6 to 1 before 35,461 fans. In the third inning Goslin drove a long homer into the right field seats for the Senators' only run. The rest of the game was wrapped up in the Giants' sixth when they scored all their runs. Moore opened with a single, only the third hit off Crowder. Terry sliced a double to left. Ott was walked intentionally, and Lefty O'Doul was sent up to pinch-hit. Lefty came through with the big hit, a sharp single through the box to put the Giants ahead 2 to 1. Just a few years ago, the impish O'Doul confided, "You know, that was an illegal hit. I wasn't going to let Crowder throw one by me so I crowded the plate closer with each pitch. On the pitch I got my hit on, I actually stepped across the plate and was afraid the umpire would call me out. But fortunately he didn't see it, nor did anybody on the Senators."

The Series moved to Washington for the third game with the attendance held to 25,727 (almost 2,000 under Griffith Stadium's capacity) by a steady drizzle which lasted until game time. President Franklin D. Roosevelt, then in the eighth month of his momentous first term in office, attended the game. He made an imposing entrance, entering Griffith Stadium by automobile through a runway as the players and an Army band stood at attention. Onlookers not given either to ceremonial pomp or to FDR's policies nevertheless had to be impressed by the famous Roosevelt luck. As the President's limousine arrived, as if on cue the drizzle stopped and the sun came out. Senator owner Clark Griffith was overheard greeting FDR with, "We're glad you're here, Mr. President, and we hope to win this one for you." Always the consummate politician, the Chief Executive threw his head back in a characteristically jaunty gesture, smiled, and responded, "Wait a minute, Clark. I'm neutral. Don't forget, I may be living in Washington now, but I'm from New York."

The Senators then beat Fitzsimmons 4 to 0 behind a masterful five-hitter by Earl Whitehill. The Washington lefty handled Terry, Ott, and Moore with ease, holding the lefthand-hitting trio hitless. Fitzsimmons yielded three runs in the first two innings with Myer, Goslin, Schulte, and Bluege getting the big hits. Fat Freddy settled down after that, but the Giants were never in the game.

The Giants were not depressed by the loss. As Terry put it, "I've said all along that pitching will dominate the Series. They got it today and we didn't. I still think our pitching will pull us through. I expect Hub will put us back in the groove tomorrow."

Hubbell faced Monte Weaver the next day before a crowd of 27,762. The game was uneventful until the top of the fourth when, with no one on, Terry drove a towering blast into the center field bleachers. Fred Schulte appeared to have a chance for the catch, but the ball just cleared a three-foot fence in front of the temporary bleachers.

29

In the Washington sixth there was some excitement although no runs scored. Manush was called out on a close play on a grounder fielded by Critz behind the diving Terry and thrown to Hubbell covering at first base. The ball, Manush, and Hubbell all seemed to arrive at the bag simultaneously. Umpire Charley Moran called the runner out, precipitating a mighty argument from the Senators that lasted for some time. At the end of the inning, after continued beefing from the Senator bench, Moran ejected Manush from the game. Apparently not believing he would be thrown out of such an important game, Heinie trotted out to his position. But Moran, backed by his three colleagues, finally convinced Manush, who nevertheless made a frenzied charge at Moran before the Senators forced him back into the dugout and clubhouse.

The Senators tied the game in the seventh when Kuhel reached base on Hubbell's error, was sacrificed to second by Bluege, and scored on Sewell's hit. The tense game continued into the eleventh inning when the Giants moved ahead on Jackson's bunt single, Mancuso's sacrifice, and Ryan's single.

In the bottom of the tenth, Washington loaded the bases with one out. Cronin sent up reserve catcher Cliff Bolton to hit for Jack Russell, who had relieved Weaver in the top of the inning and given up Ryan's go-ahead hit. The Giants conferred at the mound to decide how to play Bolton, a hard-hitting lefthand batter but an extremely slow runner. Giant reserve infielder Chuck Dressen had managed Bolton at Nashville in 1932, and Terry called him out to join the confab. But the most active participant appeared to be Blondy Ryan, who gestured vigorously as he talked to Terry. It was assumed that Terry would follow standard strategy for such a situation—play the infield in to cut down the tying run at the plate.

Finally, with the crowd at a fever pitch, the conference ended. The fans were surprised as Ryan and Critz played back for the double play, a risky maneuver. Bolton stepped up and worked Hubbell to a 3 and 2 count. The next pitch came in low and outside and Bolton clubbed a deep bouncer to Ryan. Blondy glided to his right, scooped up the ball, and flipped it to Critz. Hughie pivoted neatly and fired to Terry for the game-ending double play.

In the clubhouse, an exhausted Terry heaped praise on Hubbell but was ecstatic over Ryan and Critz. "It was Blondy and Hughie who convinced me to play Bolton the way we did," said Terry. "With the bases loaded I wanted to play in and get the force at the plate. Blondy suggested that Jackson and I play in and he and Critz play back. Ryan promised me he'd get the double play if Bolton hit to him, and I went along with him. Blondy came through and, boy, am I glad that I took his advice!"

The next day Schumacher faced Crowder before 28,454 in what proved to be another thriller. The Giants scored two runs in the third inning on a two-run single by Schumacher and another run in the sixth on doubles by

Davis and Mancuso. Fred Schulte tied the game at 3-all in the bottom of the sixth with a home run with Cronin and Manush on base. Luque came in to relieve Schumacher and managed to hold off the Senators by retiring Sewell to end the inning with two runners on.

The game settled down to a tense pitching duel between Luque and Jack Russell, who replaced Crowder in the sixth. Inning after inning went by without a serious scoring threat until the top of the tenth. Critz opened with a fly to left and Terry bounced out to second. Only Ott remained to be retired. He had fanned his first two times up and lifted easy fly balls on the next two. On a 2 and 2 count Ott cocked his right leg and lifted a long drive toward the center field bleachers. Schulte, moving back at top speed, got his glove on the ball just as it was about to drop into the low, temporary seats in front of the permanent stands. But the ball bounced out of Schulte's glove as he disappeared from sight after toppling over the low fence. Second base umpire Cy Pfirman at first ruled the drive a double, undoubtedly influenced by Cronin who kept shouting, "It's a double; it's got to be two bases on that one." Incredulous, the Giants carried their protest to umpires Moran and Moriarity. After a conference, Moran and Moriarity overruled Pfirman, and Ott was awarded the home run. That proved to be the game and Series as Luque retired the Senators in the bottom of the inning, striking out Kuhel with a flourish for the final out. The surprising Giants were the new World Champions.

Terry was almost too tired to talk after the game. "What can I say?" was his greeting in the clubhouse. Referring to the Yankees' dominance in World Series competition, he continued, "I guess we gave our league something to celebrate over after all these years. Luque and Ott did it. But still, the Series went as I expected. We had the pitching and good pitching will always do the job, particularly in a short series."

Cronin had little to say. Many years later, though, when he was President of the American League, he discussed it with a writer. "Sure I knew it was a home run but I just had to kick about it," he said. Cronin laughed. "I just didn't want to believe it, for one thing. And then, too, sometimes the umpire buys your argument and you get a break. After all, Pfirman held Ott on second before waving him around."

McGraw, aging and in failing health, had been an inconspicuous figure since his retirement. Still, he was exhilarated by the success of the club. He was proud of Hubbell's exploits and the heroics of Ott, who was the apple of his eye. But he talked mostly of Terry, his handpicked successor. "Bill did a wonderful job for us," he chortled. "At times the Senators seemed to be in a fog and Cronin just couldn't bring them out of it. With our pitching, Mel's hitting, and Terry handling the plays faultlessly, I never doubted we'd win."

The players scattered on that triumphant note. Hubbell, Fitzsimmons, Schumacher, and Parmelee—the "Big Four"—remained in town negotiating for the inevitable vaudeville offers which were traditional for Series winners in those pre-TV days. Ott's sole concern was to get "back to the folks in Gretna" and, as it turned out, to accept a surprise award—his high school diploma, presented to him eight years after he had quit school prematurely to join the Giants. Luque left immediately for his native Cuba. Critz returned to his avid fans in Greenwood, Mississippi, to describe that clutch double play on Cliff Bolton. Ryan departed for a big hometown welcome in Lynn, Massachusetts. And so it went.

Terry left New York a few days later, savoring a new $40,000, five-year player-manager contract to go with his laurels as leader of the World Champions. To top it off, an Associated Press poll voted the Giants' World Series triumph as the top team victory of 1933.

5

Heartbreak at Coogan's Bluff

The major leagues were holding their annual business meetings in New York in January 1934, and several of the writers talked with Terry at the Hotel Roosevelt. Terry was high on his club's prospects, offering to "bet anybody in the room a hat we'll finish among the top three." (For some reason hats were a popular betting item in the 1930's). Finding no takers, Terry and his audience moved on to other matters, particularly the livelier ball the National League would use in 1934 and the Giants' opponents.

On the edge of the group stood the *New York Times'* Roscoe McGowen, whose regular assignment was to cover the Dodgers. In the beginning he paid little attention to the conversation. But when Terry was questioned about the other clubs, McGowen became more attentive. He asked, "How about Brooklyn, Bill?" Terry turned to him and smiled. "Brooklyn, I haven't heard anything from them. Are they still in the league?" Everybody laughed, and everybody printed the comment. Terry, never known for his subtlety, had responded lightly, but it didn't come out that way in the writers' stories.

Thousands of letters poured into the Giants' office, all of them from irate Dodger rooters. The Dodgers had left their fans cold since falling deep into the second division. But Terry's offhand comment had fired them up. Wait until the season started. Their team would show Terry whether or not Brooklyn was still in the league!

The Giants had moved their training camp to Miami Beach. Late in February, 21 Giant batterymen reported to Flamingo Park to be greeted by a broiling sun and an enthusiastic gathering of some 500 natives and tourists, many in bathing suits and other beach attire. Even then Miami Beach was a favorite winter spot for New Yorkers, and there were many ardent Giant fans in the crowd.

The next day John McGraw died, casting a pall over the camp. Terry was visibly shaken, commenting softly, "I owe everything I have to him. He made me a first baseman and then he put me in as manager. At times he appeared to be pretty harsh and severe and I had my differences with him. But all he wanted was to get the best out of us." Henry Fabian, the veteran Polo Grounds groundskeeper, wept. He had been a rookie with McGraw in 1891 in Cedar Rapids, Iowa. Coach Pancho Snyder, a catcher under McGraw during four successive pennant-winning years from 1921 to 1924, and his fellow-coach, Tom Clark, said that McGraw would be remembered particularly by the older players for his loyalty and unpublicized handouts to them after they had left the game and were down and out. Hubbell, who McGraw had picked up from the Detroit Tigers in 1928 after Manager Ty Cobb had given up on him, attributed his pitching success to McGraw's advice to keep throwing his screwball. Schumacher, one of McGraw's last pitching stars, spoke of his fiery mentor's support of the younger players despite his outbursts at their mistakes.

After earlier professing his willingness to start the season with weak-hitting George Davis in center field, Terry surprised everyone on March 24 by trading Davis to the Cards for the less agile but harder-hitting outfielder George Watkins. With the trade, it became clear that Terry had weakened in his conviction that a tight defense alone would be enough to win as had been the case in 1933. He obviously had become convinced that the livelier ball would make a big difference in 1934, and he was willing to exchange speed and fielding for more punch.

After the Giants broke camp, they began the first of their famous annual series of exhibitions with the Cleveland Indians. This would prove to be the best known and most financially successful of preseason barnstorming series of the era. The Giant-Indian tour took them through a number of southern cities in which major league baseball was rarely if ever seen— New Orleans, Baton Rouge, Meridian, Montgomery, Atlanta, Charlotte, Asheville, Nashville, and Louisville.

Of 97 writers polled by the Associated Press, 40 picked the Giants to win the pennant, 27 picked them for second, and none thought they would finish out of the first division. Hubbell opened the regular season with an effortless 6 to 1 win over the Phillies. There were four changes in the starting Giant lineup from that opening the Series the previous fall. Ryan was at second base, filling in for the injured Critz. The rejuvenated Jackson replaced Ryan at shortstop. Newly acquired George Watkins was in center field. And Paul Richards replaced Mancuso who was still weak from a winter bout with typhoid.

The Giants won their next three games, featuring sound pitching, solid hitting, and one touch of unintentional high comedy in which Bossman Terry played the fall guy. In the second game of the season against the Phils at the Polo Grounds the Giants were leading 2 to 0 in the seventh inning with a runner on first. The next batter whistled a drive off the right field wall. Ott played the ball smartly off the concrete GEM sign and winged it to cutoff man Jackson, holding the hit to a single and keeping the runner on third. But the action didn't stop there. The alert Jackson, seeing that the batter had strayed far off first base, rifled the ball to Terry. The throw hit the surprised Terry smack between the eyes, knocking him down, and the runner scrambling back to first base trampled all over the Giant manager to finish the demolition job. The action continued with half the Giants rushing to the assistance of their fallen leader, while the other half did what they could to keep the runners in check. Both groups were successful as the Giants came out of the inning with only one enemy run scoring and Terry survived, although barely breathing. The Giants won the game and Memphis Bill was back in action the following day.

Although the Giants continued to win through May, there were problems even with Mancuso back in the lineup. With heavier hitting and increased emphasis on offense back in vogue, speed on the bases was at a higher premium and the Giants' slowness afoot cost them several games. Watkins failed to hit, and Terry replaced him in center field with Ott, then considered the best right fielder in the game. The slumping Vergez gave way to Ryan. Fitzsimmons, struck by an errant fungo bat while warming up to start a game in St. Louis, missed several starts. And Parmelee was placed on the inactive list following an appendectomy, an ailment that in those days before miracle drugs and short hospital stays sidelined him for two months.

On Memorial Day the Giants beat the Dodgers in a double-header before the largest crowd ever to pack into Ebbets Field. The insults and boos that accompanied Terry's every move through the long day were an unmistakable reminder of his offhand response to Roscoe McGowen back in January. Still, the Giants beat the Dodgers twice and that was all that mattered to Terry. That and the Giants' solid position in the league standings. The club was tied with the Cubs for second place and only 1½ games behind St. Louis.

On June 6 the Giants took over first place as Hubbell beat the Braves, with Terry and Ryan getting the big hits. Carried along by the timely hitting of Terry, Moore, O'Doul, and Ott and the steady pitching of Hubbell, Joe Bowman, Fitzsimmons, and Schumacher, the Giants held their lead through June. After smashing the Braves twice on July 4, they were in first place, three games ahead of the Cubs and four games in front of the Cardinals. Things continued to look up as Parmelee rejoined the club. Ott had been reinstalled in right field and Leiber replaced Watkins in center field. The Giants appeared well set to continue their march to a second straight pennant.

Terry, as manager of the 1933 pennant winners, piloted the National League All-Stars in the second classic at the packed Polo Grounds on July

10 with Hubbell, Ott, and Jackson joining him as the Giants' representatives. The National League's 9 to 7 loss was not the story of the game. Hubbell's pitching was.

Charley Gehringer opened the game with a clean hit to center on Hubbell's first pitch. Working too carefully, the Giant lefthander walked Heinie Manush. With two men on and the menacing trio of Babe Ruth, Lou Gehrig, and Jimmy Foxx due up, Hubbell faced a classic pitcher's nightmare. Catcher Gabby Hartnett looked first at Ruth walking to the plate with his characteristic mincing stride, scanned the array of great hitters in the American League dugout, then called time and lumbered out to the mound. "Come on, Hub," exhorted the red-faced catcher, "never mind going for the corners, just throw that 'thing' (the screwball). Hell, I can't hit it and they won't either."

Hubbell's first pitch to Ruth was off the plate, but he came back with three screwballs, each of which the Bambino swung at and missed. The piano-legged Gehrig stepped up, took a ball, and then swung futilely at three screwballs. Moon-faced Jimmy Foxx distinguished himself by comparison, at least managing one foul tip in the process of missing three more screwballs. Hubbell had fanned three of the game's all-time great hitters in 12 pitches, and the Polo Grounds rocked with applause as the solemn-faced Oklahoman walked to the dugout.

With the fans still buzzing, Hubbell—still throwing that "thing" to perfection—opened the second inning by striking out two more great hitters, Al Simmons and Joe Cronin. As the fans marvelled at Hub's artistry in striking out the five musclemen in a row, Bill Dickey broke the spell with a clean hit. Then Hubbell bore down on weak hitting Lefty Gomez and struck him out to end the inning. (For years the wisecracking Gomez would brag about "being in such distinguished hitting company.") To this day, Hubbell's feat remains the most unforgettable pitching performance in All-Star game history.

On August 10 the Giants had a 4½ game lead over the Cubs and a 6½ game margin over the Cards. By Labor Day the Giants were six games ahead of the Cards and Cubs.

In September, the pace of the Giants and Cubs slowed. But the Cards (newly christened the "Gashouse Gang" because of their rough-and-ready play and appearance) suddenly turned red hot. They were sparked by Dizzy Dean who was having an amazing year, pitching a string of complete game wins in his regular starts and relieving brilliantly in between. His younger brother Paul was a revelation after a slow start. Tex Carlton was extremely effective. The offensive load was carried by Joe Medwick, first baseman Rip Collins, and manager-second baseman Frankie Frisch. Leo Durocher was a superb shortstop, and an inexperienced catcher, Bill DeLancey, gave a remarkable performance for a rookie. By September 20, with 10 games left, the Giants' lead over the Cards had been cut to 3½ games.

Fitzsimmons beat the Phillies on September 21. But this was the day when the Dean brothers led the Cards to a storied double-header win over the Dodgers at Ebbets Field. In the first game Dizzy toyed with Stengel's club, allowing no hits for seven innings and only three hits altogether. Brother Paul pitched a no-hitter in the second game. After Paul's masterpiece, Diz was credited with the tongue-in-cheek line, "Shucks, if I knowed Paul was gonna no-hit em, I'd a done the same."

By this time Terry had moved the slowed-up Jackson from short to third and replaced him with Blondy Ryan. But it did not prevent heartbreaking losses to the Braves and the Phils—the last especially tough to take because both aces, Schumacher and Hubbell, were knocked out of the box, with the Giants losing the game in the ninth when one of Luque's low-breaking curves bounced in the dirt and eluded Mancuso. After Dizzy Dean shut out the Reds on Friday, September 28, the Giants and the Cards were tied for first place with the last weekend of the season at hand.

The Giants entered the final two-game series with the Dodgers tired physically and mentally. The hitters were in a fearful slump, particularly Ott, who had not hit safely in the last four games. Hubbell, Schumacher, and Fitzsimmons were exhausted from starting games with little rest and pitching in relief between starts. The other veterans—Terry, Critz, and Jackson—were worn out by the emotional stress as well as the physical strain.

Terry probably had given very little thought to the Brooklyn fans during the season when the Giants were riding high and the Dodgers were floundering in the second division. But now, at the rain-swept Polo Grounds that final Saturday of the season, the Dodger fans were out in full force. They carried banners aimed at their arch-rival, Terry. Banners that read "BILL WHO?" Or "I WISH *YOU* WERE IN DIXIE." And the most prevalent, "YEAH, WE'RE STILL IN THE LEAGUE." They screamed and taunted all of the Giants, even the popular Ott and Jackson, who normally were cheered even at Ebbets Field. But they saved their choicest epithets for Terry, one of the most gentle being, "Is Brooklyn still in the league, Terry? You'll find out, you cocky bastard. We'll show you."

Manager Casey Stengel started Van Lingle Mungo against Parmelee. The Dodgers took a 2 to 0 lead after six innings, with Mungo driving in both runs. They increased their lead to 5 to 0 in the ninth and the Giants got their only run on George Watkins' homer. Meanwhile, out in St. Louis, Paul Dean beat the Reds easily. The Giants were one game down.

Leaving the Polo Grounds that afternoon, Stengel passed the crestfallen Terry. "I was going in to see you fellows after the game, Bill," Casey said sympathetically, "but I decided not to." Terry, exhausted by the loss, the crowd, the long season, and the overwhelming disappointment, answered bitterly, "If you had, you would have been thrown out on your butt." The battle-scarred Stengel, stung by Terry's gruff response, replied in kind. "I might have," he shot back, "but I would have taken a piece of your hide with me."

With the Giants needing a win along with a Cardinal loss to stay alive and with improved weather conditions, Sunday's game drew more than 45,000. Thousands of Dodger fans stampeded across the East River in a wild scramble to get into the Polo Grounds. Once inside, they raised a terrific din, augmented by whistles, horns, and bells. As the Giants took the field, it probably marked the first time a team making its last stand for a pennant on its home field was greeted by more jeers than shouts of encouragement. Terry as usual drew most of the fire from the Dodger fans.

Ray Benge, opening against Fitzsimmons, was routed in a four-run first inning with Terry, Mancuso, and Ryan driving in the runs. After the Dodgers scored once, Fitzsimmons restored the four-run lead with a home run. But the fired-up Dodgers fought back to tie the game at 5-all in the eighth inning, knocking out the struggling Fitzsimmons. As Schumacher, called in to relieve Fitz, was taking his warm-up throws a loud cheer went up from the Dodger fans. The Polo Grounds scoreboards fronting the right and left field stands showed the Cardinals had taken a 3 to 0 lead over the Reds in the fourth inning.

With darkness settling over Coogan's Bluff, the game moved into the tenth inning still tied. After hits by Leslie and Cuccinello put Dodgers at first and third, Terry called in Hubbell to relieve Schumacher. King Carl struck out the next hitter, then passed the second to load the bases. But disaster struck when Ryan fumbled Al Lopez' grounder to permit Sam Leslie to score with the tie-breaker, and two more runs scored on a fly ball and another hit. The Giants went down meekly in their half of the inning, and that was the game and pennant. The exuberant Dodger fans streamed out of the Polo Grounds, their season a success despite another second division finish by their club. With Dean completing a shutout of the Reds, the Giants wound up the season two games off the pace.

The Giants' breakdown came in the face of fine seasons by several of their players. Hubbell again led the league in earned-run-average with 2.30, and in walks allowed per game and saves, was second in complete games and innings pitched, and fourth in wins with 21. Schumacher was second in wins with 23, well behind Dizzy Dean's spectacular 30 victories. Ott, hitless in his last 24 at bats, tied with Rip Collins for the home run lead with 35, led in runs-batted-in with 135, and was second in total bases and runs scored. Terry was second in hits and batting average.

Most of the Giants slipped quietly out of town the next day, barely comprehending their misfortune and even less willing to talk about it. Terry, who a year before had been on top of the baseball world, had little to say. "No, I can't explain how it happened," he lamented. "The slump just came on us suddenly, and it was too late to do anything about it. But I'm not blaming anybody and I have no alibis. The Cards simply made a great finish, and I rank them above Detroit in the Series." At least the Cardinals made one of Terry's 1934 pronouncements look good by winning the seven-game World Series that followed.

In November Terry made his first move to rehabilitate the Giants when he obtained shortstop Dick Bartell from the Phillies. It cost the Giants $75,000 and four players: Ryan, Vergez, Watkins, and a young minor league righthander, John (Pretzels) Pezzullo. In Bartell the Giants were getting a fiery performer, a consistent hitter who could pull the ball, and one of the better fielding shortstops in the game. He had earned the nickname "Rowdy Richard" for his peppery play and willingness to take on all comers despite his small stature. Bartell had been a participant in several spiking incidents over the years, including two involving the Dodgers Lonny Frey and Joe Judge, and he was considered a mortal enemy in Brooklyn.

Bartell was a big hit in the 1935 spring training camp at Miami Beach. A fairly quiet little fellow off the field, his abounding enthusiasm at short seemed to rejuvenate the other veteran infielders. His wide range at short was particularly helpful to Jackson, who seemed more assured at third base and also apparently free of injuries for the first time in years. Moore and Ott, after a series of minor injuries, worked themselves into top shape and Hank Leiber began to show the form in center field and at the plate that McGraw had envisioned back in 1932. The catching was set with Mancuso the starter and Harry Danning and Paul Richards the backup men. The pitchers were the old standbys—Hubbell, Schumacher, Parmelee, Fitzsimmons—and relievers Al Smith, Luque, and Stout.

On the trip north with the Indians, the Giants toured some of the smaller southern towns as well as the larger cities—towns like McComb and Critz' hometown, Greenwood, in Mississippi and Gastonia and Hickory in North Carolina. Terry, always the shrewd businessman, had a notion that there was much unexplored territory where major league baseball could be exploited for considerable profit during spring training, and the large exhibition game crowds bore out his theory.

Picked to finish second, the Giants opened in Boston before a freezing crowd that came out to see 41-year-old Babe Ruth play his first National League game. The Babe rewarded their fortitude by leading the Braves to a 4 to 2 win over Hubbell, driving in the first run with a blistering single and blasting a 430-foot homer to drive in the other runs. To top it off, Ruth chipped in with the game's fielding gem when he raced in from deep left field to pick off a fly ball.

A week later the Giants returned the favor by beating the Braves in 11 innings before more than 47,000 fans, at that time the largest crowd ever to watch a National League opener in New York. Ott stole the big guy's thunder with a line single to drive in the winning run. The Babe went hitless, a forerunner of the career-end disappointment which would bring him to leave the Braves before the season was half over.

The Giants went on to win their first eight home games and continued to do well in May. By Memorial Day, after a double-header win over the Braves, they were solidly in first place, 4½ games ahead of the Cards and 5½ games in front of the Cubs and Pirates. Terry, Ott, Moore, and Leiber were pounding the ball. Bartell had breathed new life into his geriatric infield partners—Terry, Critz, and Jackson. Harry Danning, batting deep in the box a la Rogers Hornsby, was used more frequently to rest Mancuso. A young righthander, Clydell (Slick) Castleman, pitched impressively enough to be promoted into the Hubbell-Schumacher-Fitzsimmons-Parmelee starting rotation, and lefties Al Smith and Allyn Stout were effective in relief.

By the All-Star game (won 4 to 1 by the American League), the Giants maintained a seven-game lead over the Cards, with the Cubs and Pirates 9½ and 10 games back respectively. The Polo Grounders were well positioned for a comeback pennant win despite the loss of Fitzsimmons for the rest of the season after elbow surgery.

The Giants began their third western trip with a good series in Pittsburgh and a split in Cincinnati. But in Chicago they lost four straight to the revitalized Cubs. Charlie Grimm had benched himself in favor of 19-year-old Phil Cavarretta at first base, and Bill Herman, Billy Jurges, and Stan Hack rounded out an excellent infield. The outfield included two new regulars, Frank Demaree and Augie Galan, along with Chuck Klein, who had been obtained from the Phils in 1934. The garrulous Gabby Hartnett continued as the regular catcher. The pitching staff included holdovers Lon Warneke, Bill Lee, and Charley Root. Tex Carleton and lefty Larry French had been picked up in trades and a little southpaw, Roy Henshaw, was a pleasant surprise.

Terry's club finished the western trip in St. Louis on a high note. They won four of six games from the Cards in four broiling, humid days, losing the first two games but bouncing back to finish the western trip three games ahead of the improved Cubs and 3½ in front of the Cards. In the first game of the double-header in St. Louis which concluded the series, the Giants had a bad scare when Schumacher collapsed on the mound in the intense heat. But to the relief of the frightened players, Doctor Hyland, the Cards' team physician, packed Schumacher in ice and "brought him back from the dead," as Blondy Ryan dramatically described it.

Although the Giants returned home with their league lead whittled down drastically, Terry was not unduly concerned. From a financial standpoint the trip was a big success, with large crowds in all of the cities. And the Giants at least had held off the Cardinals, the team Memphis Bill felt he had to beat. The Giants faced a long home stand in better shape than they had been for some time. Schumacher had recovered from his frightening experience. Parmelee, who himself had almost collapsed from the heat while pitching in St. Louis, was fit. This was the time for the club to build up its lead with games against the weaker Dodgers, Phils, and Braves while the Cards, Cubs, and Pirates struggled against each other.

But the home stand was a big disappointment. The Giants could manage no better than an even split with the eastern teams, and they led the Cards by only three games as the western teams came in for the last time. This wound up a disaster for the Giants, who won only the Cincinnati series. The Cubs, beginning a tremendous stretch drive, took three straight, and the home stand ended with the Giants out of first place—½ game behind the Cards and only 2½ games ahead of the third-place Cubs.

The only light episode during the home stand came in the unhappy Cub series when popular umpire Dolly Stark, a New York City native, was given a ''day'' and presented with an automobile before a game. This was the first time anyone could recall an umpire receiving anything from the fans other than verbal abuse or a shower of fruits and vegetables—or more damaging objects—from the stands.

But there were some fans that day who did not qualify as Dolly Stark boosters. Dolly was behind the plate, and up in the stands some 25,000 leather-lunged rooters were pulling for Ott to hit one as he stood at the plate in the first inning. With a 2 and 1 count, Larry French wound up and the ball shot toward Gabby Hartnett's mitt. Stark's upraised arm indicated a called strike even before his booming voice reached the ears of the fans to announce ''Strike Two.'' Ott stepped out of the batters box and said something to Stark. The anti-Stark contingent couldn't hear what he said, but they could imagine. Immediately they took up the cry. ''Tell him, Ottie,'' came the stentorian shout, ''they should have bought him eyeglasses, not a car.''

The 2 and 2 pitch came in, and again Ott took it without swinging. Stark raised his clenched right fist again and bawled, ''You're out!'' Ott turned around, said something to Stark, then walked back to the Giant dugout in apparent disgust. For the rest of the game Stark took a merciless riding from the stands.

After the game one of the writers wandered into the umpire's dressing room. He was surprised to hear Stark laughing about the game. ''Dolly,'' the writer asked, ''remember those strikes you called on Ott when the fans started to ride you? What was it Mel said when he turned around and spoke to you?'' Stark grinned broadly. ''Oh, nothing much,'' he replied. ''Mel knew they were both strikes. The first time he said, 'Dolly, I'd give ten bucks to have that one back.' The second time he was really disgusted. He said to me, 'How can I take two beautiful pitches like that in a row?'''

As September began, the Cardinals were still in first place, two games ahead of the Giants, 2½ in front of the streaking Cubs, and eight games ahead of the Pirates. The Giants began their last crucial western swing in Cincinnati. Hubbell opened the tour by beating the Reds, his twentieth win of the season. The Giants split the next two games and then moved on to Pittsburgh where Hubbell and Castleman won two of three games against the Pirates. The Cubs continued their winning streak, climbing past the Giants into second place.

The Terrymen moved into St. Louis, 3½ games behind the Cardinals. Dizzy Dean beat Hubbell in the first game. But the Giants came back fighting. The next day Frank (Gabby) Gabler, a talkative, young rookie righthander, beat Paul Dean in an exciting 10-inning, see-saw slugging match. The following day Castleman won 5 to 4 in 11 innings, and the Cubs moved past the Cards into first place. Then Hubbell beat Dizzy Dean in a game played before an overflow crowd at Sportsmans Park with many onlookers sitting on the outskirts of the outfield separated from the players by only a clothesline.

The Giants had a few fans among the largely hostile group ringing the outfield. Ott told of three young men who were rooting for the Giants. Mel said, "It took courage but they always had something encouraging to shout to me after I took my post each inning. If I'd batted in a run, or even hit a loud foul, they would give me a little cheer. The rest of the mob squatted out there on the grass and gave 'em plenty of dirty looks and muttered threats. But these three fellows just grinned and ignored them. Late in the game the Cards worked a runner around into scoring position and Charlie Gelbert hit a long fly I had to backpedal to catch. Just as I got set to catch the ball I felt something tickle my ribs. I took my eye off the ball for a second and saw a pop bottle sail under my arm. It was the last out of the inning and naturally I turned around to see who tossed the bottle. 'Come on, Mel,' one of my buddies shouted indignantly. 'Let's get him.' The three of them went cruising around that mob, doing everything but step on faces, and I went along. But we couldn't spot anybody with a guilty look and had to give it up."

On their last stop, in Chicago, the Giants were demolished. Lon Warneke, Larry French, Charlie Root, and Bill Lee beat them with little difficulty. The Cubs were on their way to a 21-game winning streak and the Giants simply provided the 13th, 14th, 15th, and 16th victories before the Wrigley Field steamroller. Terry's club ended the trip on September 19, 7½ games behind the Cubs and 5½ in back of the Cards. They were a disappointed club although there was some slight satisfaction in having retaliated against the Cards for the last-ditch defeat Frisch's club had dealt them in 1934.

Terry, who hit well over .400 on the trip and had drawn grudging cheers from the rival fans for his brilliant play, held a press conference when the

Giants returned to New York. He announced that he was retiring as a player and was planning a drastic housecleaning. The last trip had been a bitter disappointment to him, especially after the Giants had fought back to take the last three games in St. Louis before the debacle in Chicago.

A writer asked Terry, "What's the problem and the future as you see it?" Terry replied succinctly, "The problem is too many old men. And that includes the first baseman, too. From now on, we're out only for youth and speed." He was satisfied with his three outfielders, Moore, Ott, and Leiber. Hubbell, Schumacher, Castleman, and Harry Gumbert, a lanky righthander just up from Baltimore, figured in his future plans. Bartell and Maneuso also were set although Bartell had slipped badly in the last half of the season. Travis Jackson would be retained as a utility infielder and pinch hitter. But there were three gaping holes in the infield—Terry and Critz were retiring and a new third baseman was needed.

On September 27 the Cubs capped their almost unbelievable drive, clinching the pennant with a 6 to 2 defeat of Dizzy Dean and the Cards in the first half of a double-header—their 20th consecutive victory. Their 21st straight win in the second game was anticlimactic. But the incredible streak had wiped out all opposition. The Giants finished in third place, a whopping 8½ games behind the Cubs.

Hubbell had an excellent year, winning 23 and losing 12 and finishing second in wins, strikeouts, innings pitched, and complete games. Schumacher was third in earned-run-average. Ott was second in homers behind the Braves' Wally Berger, fourth in runs-batted-in, second in total bases, and third in bases on balls. Leiber had what was to be his best year, hitting .331 and batting in 107 runs. Terry, retirement plans and all, tied for fifth in batting with a .341 average.

On October 10 the Giants, who had long resisted broadcasting their games on radio, filed a suit to restrain "bootleg" broadcasts of all sporting events from the Polo Grounds. The suit was filed against several communication companies although the Giants admitted "the method of acquiring the simultaneous description of baseball games is unknown." And on that indeterminate note, the Giants' 1935 season ended.

CARL HUBBELL

6

Pennant Winners

At the winter meeting Terry attended to one of his first priorities, a replacement for Hughie Critz who had retired. Terry's man was Burgess Whitehead, an unheralded utility infielder with the Cardinals. To get Whitehead, the Giants gave up a first-line starter, Parmelee, along with pitcher Allyn Stout, young Al Cuccinello, and Phil Weintraub. Critics of the deal conceded that Whitehead was fast, an agile second baseman who could make the double play, an occasional hitter, and a good hit-and-run man, all of which the Giants needed. But they questioned whether the slim, frail-looking Whitehead had the stamina to play a full season. Even the doubters, though, were intrigued by the Tarboro, North Carolina, native who had graduated Phi Beta Kappa from the University of North Carolina—hardly a prequisite to being a member of the rough-and-ready Gas House Gang.

Failing in attempts to trade for an established first baseman, Terry re-acquired Sam Leslie from the Dodgers just before spring training opened at Pensacola, Florida. The only other experienced players picked up were pitcher Dick Coffman from the Browns and ancient reliever Firpo Marberry, who had labored for the Tigers after several big years with the Senators.

On January 6, 1936, President Charles Stoneham died. He was the only survivor of the triumvirate which had purchased the Giants in 1919, the other two members being McGraw and Magistrate Francis X. McQuade. An important Wall Street figure in the 1920's, Stoneham had been an unobtrusive club president with his aggressive partner, McGraw, running the club with an iron hand until June 1932 and the less flamboyant but equally strong-willed Terry calling the shots since then. A week later, 32-year-old Horace Stoneham replaced his father. Leo Bondy became vice-president in addition to his previous duties as treasurer. A few weeks later the popular Eddie Brannick, who had been associated with the Giants since he was a small boy, became the team secretary.

Whitehead made an unusual entrance at training camp, carrying a tennis racket with his luggage. One of the case-hardened McGraw era coaches was heard to mutter, "What the hell does he think we're down here training for, a pennant race or Wimbledon?" But very soon Whitehead impressed everybody favorably, working smoothly with Bartell, handling the bat cleverly, and moving with exceptional grace. Jimmy Ripple, a chunky young outfielder from Export, Pennsylvania, also looked good with his lefthand power and determination.

Just before the season opened, National League President Ford Frick announced a new "nonfraternization" rule. Under this edict, opposing team players were forbidden to talk to each other on the field. To make the rule even more ridiculous, if caught fraternizing (a term that would take on a more interesting meaning in World War II), both the player and his manager were subject to fines.

Picked to finish behind the Cubs and the Cardinals, the Giants opened the season in fine style, reeling off five straight victories against the Dodgers and the renamed, but unimproved, Boston Bees. With Leslie at first and Travis Jackson at third, the Giants won three action-packed games with the Dodgers at the Polo Grounds. In the second game, Van Mungo and Bartell became involved in a manner not to be confused with the fraternization that Frick had in mind. Bartell grounded to first baseman Buddy Hassett for what appeared to be a routine, unassisted putout by Hassett. Mungo, coming over to cover the bag, appeared to give Dick a hard jolt with his hip. From a bleacher vantage point, Bartell seemed to fly through the air as though shot out of a cannon. He turned a couple of somersaults and landed flat on his back.

Without stopping for a breather the peppery Bartell scrambled to his feet. He screamed at Mungo, "You did that on purpose, you lousy son of a bitch." Almost simultaneously the two men charged each other and began flailing away, with the much larger pitcher falling on top of Bartell. The dugouts emptied quickly. Umpire Beans Reardon raced over from third base and, knee deep in ballplayers, finally succeeded in prying apart the two battlers. Then he booted both men out of the game.

The next day both Bartell and Mungo were fined $25. Frick announced, almost apologetically, "The fines were the smallest for a fist fight in a good many years. I made them small because there are degrees of fights. This one was not premeditated. No one got hurt and no one even got a black eye." (Apparently this was the acid test.)

But that was not the end of Mungo's problems that day. Pitching in relief, he lost in the bottom of the ninth on a freak play which showed the Dodgers had not lost their flair for serio-comedy. Winning 6 to 5 with two out and no one on base, Mungo walked Whitehead and gave up a single to

Ott. Leiber popped a fly into short left, apparently an easy game-ending out. The veteran Freddy Lindstrom, just picked up by the Dodgers after a distinguished career with the Giants and the Pirates, trotted in easily to make the catch. Uncharacteristically, he crashed head-on into shortstop Jimmy Jordan as Jordan drifted back and reached up for the ball. The ball bounced out of Jordan's glove and both men tumbled to the ground dazed. Whitehead and Ott, running with two out, scored the tying and winning runs. Later, in the clubhouse, Lindstrom said unbelievingly, "I've been in the league for 12 years and that never happened to me until I became a Dodger." Mungo's postgame comments were unquotable.

Before the Giants' first appearance of the year at Ebbets Field, Terry requested extra police protection, and 20 additional officers were assigned to the ball park. There was some suspicion that the request was designed, in part at least, to exploit the traditional Giant-Dodger rivalry as Bartell was ill and unable to play. All of the excitement was confined to the see-saw game which the Dodgers won in the tenth on a pinch hit by an obscure rookie catcher, one Sidney Gautreaux.

On Memorial Day the Giants surprisingly were only 1½ games behind the league-leading Cardinals as Terry manipulated his troops masterfully. Leiber, in a bad slump after his fine 1935 season, was platooned in center field with Jimmy Ripple. Leslie also slumped and Terry, still on the roster, took over at first base for a few games. Jackson, slowed up perceptibly, shared third base with Eddie Mayo, up from Baltimore. Only Whitehead and Bartell held the infield together with their consistent, sparkling play. Hubbell was superb, but the other pitchers were under par and Castleman, in particular, was a bitter disappointment after his fine rookie year.

By the All-Star game break, the Giants had dropped to fifth place, although they were only 5½ games behind the first-place Cubs. In the All-Star game, the National League won for the first time, 4 to 3, on Augie Galan's disputed home run which struck the right field foul pole at Braves Field in Boston. Hubbell, Ott, Moore, and Terry were picked to represent the Giants, although Terry had to bow out to visit his doctor in Memphis, where he was told that his ailing knee made further play inadvisable.

When Terry returned it was widely believed that his playing days were over. The Giants' first base situation was up in the air. Sam Leslie had been erratic at bat and his play at the bag had not improved. One possibility that Terry considered briefly was to bring up young Norman (Babe) Young, a recent Fordham University graduate, just beginning his minor league apprenticeship with the Giants' Greenwood, Mississippi, farm club. Another possibility was to try Leiber at first base, but Terry also discarded this idea. For better or worse, Leslie apparently would be the regular first baseman for the rest of the season.

After losing the first game of a double-header to the Pirates on July 15, the Giants' pennant hopes touched bottom. They were 11 games behind the league-leading Cubs and were lodged in fifth place, nearer to sixth than fourth. But they took the second game as Terry, playing on his crippled left knee against his doctor's advice, led the club with a single, double, and triple. The next day Ott's eighth inning home run retrieved a come-from-behind win over the Pirates. Hubbell, helped by a record-tying four Giant triples in one inning, shut out the Pirates in the last game of the series to give the club another boost. After taking two out of three from the Reds, the Giants returned home in fourth place, 9½ games behind the Cubs. The club continued its resurgence against the western clubs at the Polo Grounds and wound up the home stand only 5½ games out of first place.

The Giants stepped up their pace, winning 17 of the next 18 games. Their performance was marked by Hubbell's sensational pitching, Ott's clutch hitting, and the play of their two crippled first basemen—the courageous Leslie who played with a severely pulled groin muscle and Terry who played sporadically but effectively.

The final western trip began in Cincinnati with the Giants on a winning streak and only half a game behind the league-leading Cardinals. The Polo Grounders moved into first place when Leiber beat the Reds with a late inning hit. In Pittsburgh, Fitzsimmons won over Waite Hoyt in the fourteenth inning when Terry came off the coaching line to belt a pinch-hit single. The next day the Pirates' Red Lucas broke the Giants' 15-game winning streak. But the Giants came back to take a double-header in Chicago, highlighted by Hubbell's twentieth victory (his seventh straight) and Ott's dramatic ninth inning homer topping off his seven-hit day. The trip ended successfully with Hubbell beating Dizzy Dean 2 to 1 and driving in the winning run. The Giants returned home triumphantly with a four-game lead over the second-place Cardinals. Since their comeback on July 15 they had won 39 of 47, a cool .830 pace.

On Labor Day the Giants took two games from the Phillies and moved five games ahead of St. Louis. With their closest competitors finishing on the road and the Giants home for most of the remainder of the season, Terry's club was in a strong position—if the players could forget their shattering experiences in 1934 and 1935.

The western clubs came in for the last time, and the Giants held their own against the Cubs and the Reds. The Cards were next and the Giants managed to hold them off, splitting a double-header before a full house at the Polo Grounds. There was a play in the second game that was strictly out of the old, daffy Dodgers' playbook. Cardinal rookie pitcher Cotton Pippen was the runner at second base and Terry Moore was on first when another rookie, Art Garibaldi, smashed a line drive to deep right center. It looked like a certain double or triple until the hard-to-understand, Cuban third base coach, Mike Gonzales, got into the act. (Gonzales had gained his share of baseball immortality with his memorable scouting report on a young prospect—"Good field, no hit.") As Pippen and Moore ran the bases they became hopelessly confused by a series of staccato orders shrieked by Gonzales in his best pidgin English "Go, go! You stay! Hol' up, hol' up!" Pippen stopped uncertainly halfway between third and home. At the same time Moore rounded second and raced for third until he saw the thoroughly confused Pippen becalmed between third and home. Meanwhile, Ott's throw came in from deep right field and Pippen was tagged out between third and home, with Moore caught between second and third. Garibaldi, equally befuddled, retreated uncertainly to first. The Cardinals had succeeded in converting an apparent two-run double or triple with none out into a mere single and a double play with no runs in. Leo Durocher reported that after that loss Manager Frankie Frisch berated the team in the locked clubhouse for nearly three hours.

The Giants won the rubber game of the Cardinal series to move 4½ games ahead of the Cards and six games in front of the Cubs. Both Hubbell and Dizzy Dean relieved the starting pitchers, and Hub wound up with his 24th win of the season. The Cards added their own brand of spice to the game with a free-swinging brawl on their bench between Joe Medwick and pitcher Ed Heusser. Since this was a private Gas House Gang fight, in the relative privacy of their dugout although in clear public view, the umpires studiously ignored the brawl until the Cards themselves separated their battling teammates.

Terry's club clinched the pennant in Boston on September 24 when Schumacher outpitched Danny MacFayden and drove in the winning run. The Giants finished the season with a 92 and 62 record, five games ahead of the Cards and the Cubs who tied for second.

Hubbell had a remarkable year and was voted the Most Valuable Player in the league. He had 16 consecutive wins as the campaign ended, led the league in wins (26), winning percentage, and in earned-run-average. Over and above his imposing statistics, though, King Carl's true value was best reflected by his ability to win the important games and to give stability to the pitching staff when the older pitchers slumped and the younger pitchers floundered.

Ott had one of his best years, leading the league in homers (36) and slugging percentage, and finishing near the top in runs-batted-in, runs scored, and bases on balls. He, like his roommate and close friend, Hubbell, was a blue chip performer all season, particularly in late inning, clutch situations.

Jo-Jo Moore had a great year, leading off effectively and playing brilliantly in the field. Mancuso had a fine year and was given much of the credit for the pitching staff's late-season resurgence. And Bartell and Whitehead proved to be the best second base-shortstop combination the Giants had in many years. Their play was especially important for the kind of low score, defense-oriented style of play that was the Giants' hallmark. Whitehead, incidentally, played in all 154 games, an effective rebuttal to the critics who thought he lacked the stamina to play regularly.

The Giants and their fans luxuriated in the pennant win for a few days. Then their thoughts turned to the World Series with the powerful Yankees, as New York prepared for the first "nickel," subway World Series between the Giants and Yanks since 1923. The 1936 Yankees unquestionably were one of the all-time great ball clubs, compared favorably by many experts to the 1927 Yankees of "Murderers' Row" fame. Joe McCarthy's team had made a shambles of the American League race, clinching the pennant as early as September 9 and going on to win by an overwhelming 19½ games over the second-place Detroit Tigers. The Yanks had everything—a crushing hitting attack, great defense, and an excellent pitching staff.

At first base Lou Gehrig was the greatest home run hitter of the day and a dependable fielder. Veteran second baseman Tony Lazzeri could still do the job in the field and hit the long ball. Frankie Crosetti was a spry shortstop, a good leadoff man, and capable of hitting for distance on occasion. Third baseman Red Rolfe was a proficient number 2 hitter, a skilled bunter, and a sound fielder.

The outfield was dominated by young Joe DiMaggio. The graceful rookie's marvelous year had exceeded the rave notices he brought to the Yanks from the experts who had observed him in the Pacific Coast League. Right fielder George (Twinkletoes) Selkirk, finally overcoming the burden he carried as Babe Ruth's successor, was a good hitter and outfielder although he was overshadowed by the superstars on the club. In the other outfield slot Jake Powell, obtained during the season from the Senators, was an adequate performer. Lanky Bill Dickey, then in his prime, had long been recognized as one of the great catchers. He was an excellent receiver and thrower, a fine handler of pitchers, and one of the game's most consistent hitters with his classic level swing.

The pitching staff was deep and well balanced. Big, rugged Charley (Red) Ruffing was the leading righthand starter. Lefty Gomez was an excellent pitcher, particularly effective in important games. Ex-Indian and Senator Monte Pearson, Irving (Bump) Hadley, and Yale graduate Johnny Broaca were the other regular starters. Ex-Chicago Cub Pat Malone did double duty as a starter and reliever. Johnny (Grandma) Murphy, a Fordham University alumnus (and many years later general manager of the New York Mets), was one of the leading relief pitchers of the day.

The Yanks held a wide hitting edge over the Giants. They had set a new major league record for club home runs with 182, including a league-leading 49 by Gehrig, 29 by DiMaggio, and 22 by Dickey. Even more remarkable was their feat of having five regulars—Gehrig, DiMaggio, Dickey, Lazzeri, and Selkirk—who had driven in more than 100 runs. By comparison in the entire National League only six players had exceeded the 100 RBI mark and Ott was the only Giant who had done so. This was a distribution of power that threatened to put a terrific strain upon the Giant pitchers.

The widespread interest in the Series was reflected in the heavy betting before the opener. Oddsmaker Jack Doyle, the Jimmy the Greek of his day, pronounced the Yanks a prohibitive favorite to win the Series although the Giants were strong favorites in the opener with Hubbell pitching.

The first game was played at the Polo Grounds with Hubbell facing Ruffing. It was played in a steady downpour on a rain-soaked field before 39,419 drenched onlookers. Selkirk and Bartell hit solo homers, then the Giants went ahead 2 to 1 in the sixth inning when Mancuso drove in Ott.

Hubbell had no real trouble until the Yankee eighth. Crosetti doubled and Rolfe was safe on his sacrifice bunt when Hubbell slipped fielding it on the wet grass. With none out, DiMaggio lashed a screwball on a low line toward right field. Whitehead moved quickly to his left, speared the ball just off the ground, and doubled Rolfe off first base. Encouraged by that break, Hubbell retired Dickey to end the inning. In the bottom of the eighth, the Giants put the game away with a four-run burst on a bases-filled walk to Whitehead, Jackson's sacrifice fly, and a scratch hit by Hubbell which the Yanks mishandled.

In the clubhouse there was unanimous agreement that Whitehead's play on DiMaggio's liner was the key play of the game. As Terry put it, "It meant the difference for them between at least having the tying run in, men on first and second or third and nobody out, compared with no runs, two out, and only a man on third."

Schumacher opposed Gomez in the second game before a crowd of 43,543 including President Roosevelt, who was in New York campaigning for his second term. The Yanks, unhampered by such obstacles as Hubbell's artistry, inclement weather, and poor field conditions, tore into Schumacher and four other Giant pitchers in a 17-hit, 18 to 4 slaughter in which every Yankee got at least one hit. Lazzeri hit a grand-slam home run in a seven-run, third-inning outburst, and Tony, along with Bill Dickey, batted in five runs.

The most interesting play of the one-sided game was contributed by DiMaggio. The Californian made a stunning, game-ending catch on a prodigious blast by Leiber. Hank drove the ball almost directly in front of the Eddie Grant Memorial tablet in deepest center field at the base of the clubhouse. DiMag turned at the crack of the bat, looking first over one shoulder and then the other, and raced well beyond the bleacher screens. He made the catch with his back half turned to the plate some 475 feet away, then casually trotted up the steps to the visiting team's clubhouse as the remaining onlookers looked on in amazement.

Moving to the Yankee Stadium for the third game, it was Fitzsimmons against Bump Hadley in a tight game before 64,842, the largest crowd to attend a World Series game up to that time. Fitz was in good form and the Yanks touched him for only four hits while the Giants collected 11. Still, the power-packed Bombers eked out a 2 to 1 win on a deflected infield hit by Crosetti that the acrobatic Whitehead could not handle.

In the fourth game it was Hubbell against Monte Pearson before 66,669, another new Series attendance record. The Yanks scored one run in the second and three more in the third on Gehrig's booming homer into the bleachers. The Giants came back to score a run in the fourth when Ripple drove in Bartell. Hubbell held the Yanks after that but left the game after the seventh inning, behind 4 to 1. The Giants could do little against Pearson and lost 5 to 2.

After the game Terry talked about his knee ailment. He said that he had been confined to his hotel room except when he was at the ball park, sleeping at night with pillows under his left leg to reduce the swelling. He told the writers, "I'm playing out this string, but you can bet anything that I'll never play again after this is over."

Schumacher faced Ruffing the next day in the fifth game before 50,024. Although loosely played, this was by far the most exciting game of the Series. Tied at 4-all after nine tense innings, Moore opened the tenth inning with a double and moved to third on Bartell's sacrifice. Terry then lifted a towering fly to DiMaggio to bring in Moore. The tenacious Schumacher held the Yanks in the bottom of the inning, and the Terrymen had reduced the Yanks' lead in games to 3 to 2.

In the sixth game Fitzsimmons faced Gomez on a gray, murky afternoon at the Polo Grounds with 38,427 on hand. By the fifth inning, the Yanks had taken a 5 to 2 lead and driven out Fitzsimmons. The Giants fought back in the seventh, but Johnny Murphy relieved Gomez and struck out pinchhitter Mark Koenig to end the inning with the go-ahead Giant run on base.

All that followed was anticlimactic. The Yanks went ahead 6 to 4 in the eighth and broke the game wide open in the ninth. Before they were retired, 13 Yanks had batted and seven had scored, increasing their lead to 13 to 5. The Giants went down meekly in the ninth, and the Yankees were the new World Champions.

In the victorious Yankee clubhouse McCarthy was magnanimous. "The Giants are a much better ball club than people give them credit for. They gave us a whale of a battle." Terry could still smile. Perhaps he thought his club had done well to carry the Series to six games. "That's the toughest club I ever faced," said Bill. "They have everything. And who told me they didn't have a good pitching staff? They're just a great team."

In a rare show of sentimentality, Terry talked about Travis Jackson who had shown his age during the season and particularly during the

Series. "I wouldn't take him out of the Series," said Memphis Bill. "I thought he deserved to play after the kind of ball he has given this club for years. But next year? No, Jax can't go another season."

Pirate manager Pie Traynor lauded Terry, who had played through the entire Series as a virtual cripple. Traynor added, "I don't think any other man in baseball could have finagled that team into a World Series. For that matter, he did well to win a game, let alone two games, against a powerhouse like the Yanks." There were few Giant fans who didn't agree with Traynor.

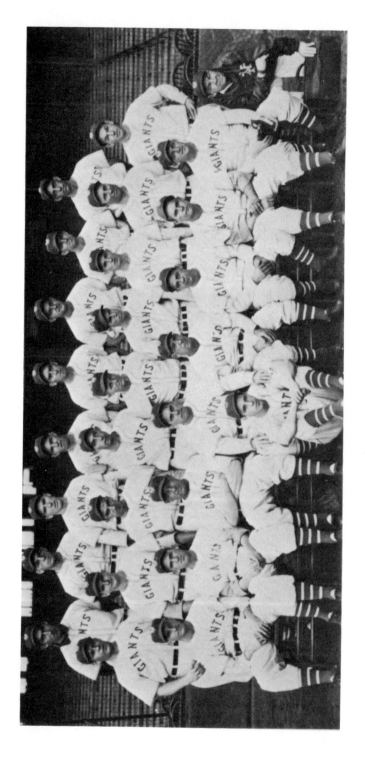

NEW YORK GIANTS—1937 NATIONAL LEAGUE CHAMPIONS

Back row: Harry Danning, Hal Schumacher, Jimmy Ripple, Mel Ott, Al Smith, Eddie Madjeski, Dick Bartell, Lou Chiozza; **center row:** Hank Leiber, Tom Baker, Carl Hubbell, Cliff Melton, Dick Coffman, Harry Gumbert, Johnny McCarthy, Wally Berger, Blondy Ryan; **front row:** Burgess Whitehead, Joe Moore, Frank Snyder (coach), Bill Terry (manager), Dolph Luque (coach), Gus Mancuso, Sam Leslie, Don Brennan, Willie Schaeffer (trainer); **in front,** Tom Troy (mascot).

7

Two in a Row

For several years the Giants had relied upon trades to restaff the team. But now with Terry and Jackson retired and the years taking their toll of some of the other McGraw-era holdovers, it was clear that the Giants had to build up their meager farm system to compete with teams such as the Cardinals and the Yankees with their extensive, flourishing farm clubs. With this in mind, just before 1936 ended the Giants purchased the Albany club of the Triple-A International League for $50,000. Then they transferred the franchise to nearby Jersey City and installed Travis Jackson as manager.

The new players of note obtained during the offseason were lefthander Cliff Melton, up from Baltimore, and utility infielders Lou Chiozza from the Phils and Tommy Thevenow from the Reds. With the Giants unable to obtain an established first baseman, that position was up for grabs among fancy-fielding Johnny McCarthy, who had been brought up from Newark late in the 1936 season, old faithful Sam Leslie, and Les Powers, purchased from Baltimore.

The spring training period was split between Havana, Cuba, and Gulfport, Mississippi. On the barnstorming tour north, the main attraction was the Indians' young righthander, Bob Feller, who had been sensational since joining Cleveland during the 1936 season. Feller made believers out of the Giants in his first outing against them in Vicksburg, Mississippi, striking out a number of them handily with his blinding speed and sharp curve. Bartell alone was unimpressed, commenting, "Heck, Van Mungo's definitely quicker and we've got several other guys in our league who can throw as fast."

Hank Leiber unfortunately became the Giants' foremost authority on the velocity of Feller's fast ball when the Iowa youngster beaned him in a game in New Orleans. This was long before batting helmets came into use, and Leiber went down like a felled steer. Although the big Arizonan escaped a skull fracture he was sidelined with severe head ailments for most of the campaign.

The tour with the Indians took the two teams, traveling in style in eight Pullman cars and private dining and club cars, through the Deep South, Texas, Oklahoma, and on into New York. Throughout, Feller continued to impress, and frighten, the Giants with his lightning speed. As if in response to Bartell's putdown, Feller seemed to bear down especially hard against the little shortshop, fanning him 13 times in 18 at-bats. As Bill Corum of the *Journal-American* summed it up, "Bartell had to go all the way from Vicksburg to Charlotte before he got so much as a loud foul against the kid."

The Giants and Dodgers opened the season at Ebbets Field in typically explosive fashion. Bartell, leading off against Mungo, took the first pitch across the letters for a strike. As he turned around to protest the call to Umpire Beans Reardon, he was hit squarely in the chest by an overripe tomato which came flying out of the stands behind first base. Rowdy Richard took this splattering with commendable aplomb, and the game continued after an extended towelling off period. A few days later at the Polo Grounds, hard feelings between the clubs boiled over as Bartell tagged Dodger infielder Jimmy Bucher with more vigor than Bucher considered necessary. Both men bounced to their feet and squared off as both squads raced onto the field. But after the usual heated words and threatening gestures, the umpires restrained the would-be combatants and the game continued.

The Giants, minus the headache-plagued Leiber, were in third place as they arrived in St. Louis to begin their first western swing. In the first bout against the Cardinals Hubbell defeated Dizzy Dean in a game marked by a monumental brawl involving almost all of the players. Trouble began brewing in the sixth inning when a balk, called by Umpire George Barr against Dean, helped the Giants to a three-run inning, wiping out a Cardinal lead. Facing Bartell with one out and Whitehead on second, Dean half turned toward second and then, without coming to the prescribed pause in his delivery, pitched to Bartell who lifted an easy fly ball for the apparent second out. But Barr disallowed the play and called a balk on Dean for failing to pause a full second in his delivery. Given another chance, Bartell lined to Pepper Martin in right field. The colorful Pepper, busy preparing a fresh chaw of tobacco with his glove tucked under one arm, could not get his guard up fast enough and muffed the ball. Whitehead scored and Dean fumed out on the mound. The Giants scored two more runs during the inning as Dean's temper rose to the boiling point.

Dizzy took out his anger on the Giants. He began to throw bean balls, pitches thrown not so much to keep hitters loose at the plate but rather to force them to hit the dirt to avoid being skulled. Batter after batter the

Giants went up and down like duckpins. An angry shouting match continued for several innings between Dean and the Giants. The climax came in the ninth, when Dean sent Ripple sprawling to avoid a pitch headed for his chin. Climbing to his feet, Ripple looked into the Giant dugout, nodded as if giving his teammates a signal, then shouted to Dean, "The next one is going down the line, you hillbilly bastard! Let's see if you've got the guts to cover."

With that, Ripple bunted well inside the first base line. The ball, hit harder than Ripple had intended, bounded to second baseman Jimmy Brown, who prepared to throw it to Mize at first. But Brown held the ball as Dean, who no longer had any business in the play, raced over to first base determined to block the stocky Ripple's path to the bag. The two men crashed right on the base. Almost simultaneously, the Giants poured out to the mound where they were joined by the entire Cardinal team. Fists flew wildly, and for a time it was difficult to tell the fighters from the peacemakers. Off to one side, near the backstop, Gus Mancuso and Mickey Owen became embroiled in their own private slugfest.

Eventually Umpires Barr, Dolly Stark, and Bill Stewart and a squad of policemen managed to separate the battlers. Surprisingly, the umpires evicted only Mancuso and Owen, presumably because they had started a private fight. The ruffled but otherwise uninjured Dean and Ripple were allowed to remain in the game, and Ripple was credited with a single as, in all the excitement, he had never been put out at first. Equally surprising, considering the number of players involved, the only reported injury was a magnificent black eye administered to Cardinal rookie third baseman Don Gutteridge by doughty Dolph Luque. Through it all the serene Hubbell, the only player to remain quietly on the sidelines, moved along imperturbably to win his sixth straight victory of the campaign and his 22nd in a row (not counting his World Series loss to the Yankees).

The next day Ford Frick fined Dean and Ripple for starting the brawl, but not Mancuso or Owen despite their ejection from the game. Manager Frankie Frisch would not answer Frick directly when asked whether Dean had thrown bean balls. And Terry's only comment was a solicitous "We all feel sorry about little Gutteridge's black eye."

In Chicago Terry benched Ott, who was batting a dismal .167, and replaced him with Ripple. (Ott had tried everything to shake his season-long slump, including switching back to his old familiar number 4 uniform after having been assigned the retired Terry's Number 3.) This was the first time Ott had been benched for not hitting since he became a regular in 1928. It was not the immediate solution as the Giants lost to the Cubs the next day. But the following day Ott's brief rest cure ended, and he responded by supplying all of the power in a victory over the Cubs with a three-run homer off Larry French, one of his favorite "cousins." Mel also hit homers to provide the winning margins in succeeding series as Hubbell beat the Pirates and the Reds to run his consecutive game-winning streak to 24. Sparked by their two leaders, the Giants continued to win and returned home in second place, only 1½ games behind the league-leading Pirates.

Hubbell's winning streak came to an end at 24 at the hands of his old nemesis, the Dodgers, in the first game of the Memorial Day double-header. The second largest crowd in Polo Grounds history, 61,756, watched as King Carl was routed in the fourth inning after retiring only one batter. But it was not Hub's last appearance of the day. Between games of the double-header he stood at home plate to receive the 1936 National League Most Valuable Player award. It was presented to him by a portly, snappily dressed Babe Ruth, a man still waiting in unhappy leisure for an offer to manage a major league team.

Towering Cliff Melton, who had been a pleasant surprise all season, relieved Castleman in the second game and took a fearful riding from the Dodgers. Dodger shortstop Woody English, in particular, gave the toothy, guileless southpaw from North Carolina a rough time. Batting against the elephant-eared Melton, English yelled out to him, "You ought to paint those ears green." Melton drawled back, "What for?" Woody rasped in reply. "To give us a good batting background, you busher!" The good-natured lefty grinned sheepishly. But he had the last laugh. He was the winning pitcher when Johnny McCarthy singled in the winning run in the last of the ninth to give the Giants an even split on the day.

The club held its own in June as Hubbell, Schumacher, Melton, and Castleman pitched steady ball; Mancuso, Bartell, and Whitehead anchored the defense; and Ott regained his hitting form.

The Giants made two trades before the June 15 trading deadline. They acquired Wally Berger from Boston to supply righthand hitting power lost when Leiber went on the sidelines. A shocker came when Terry traded the veteran Fitzsimmons to the Dodgers for Tom Baker, a young right-hander. Looking back on it, this was one of the worst deals in Giant history. Baker, sent to Jersey City for more seasoning, came back to win a total of two games for the Giants before they released him in 1938. Fitzsimmons, who had done little for the Giants all season, found a new home at Ebbets Field and helped the Dodgers for several years. At the time of the trade, though, Fitz thought it was the worst day of his life. He told a writer years later, "I'll never forget riding across the bridge to Brooklyn in a taxi that afternoon. More than once I almost told the driver to turn around and go back. What was I going to Brooklyn for? I was a Giant and for years I had hated the Dodgers. It almost made me sick to think I had been traded to them. But it turned out well."

The last of the epic Hubbell-Dean pitching battles came on June 27. This one was won by King Carl in St. Louis as Ott supported him with two homers. The club returned home a game behind the first-place Cubs, a position they retained through July 4.

58

The Giants were well represented on the National League All-Star team. Terry managed the team, and Hubbell, Ott, Moore, Bartell, Whitehead, and Mancuso were on the squad. The game, played in Washington, was won by the Yankee-dominated American League team, 8 to 3.

The team slumped in July. By early August it had fallen seven games back of the league-leading Cubs, and Terry shook up the lineup in the middle of a western trip. He replaced Chiozza at third base with the versatile Ott, Leiber took over in right field with Ripple going to center field, and Sam Leslie took McCarthy's place at first. The lineup changes helped, and the Giants picked up three games on the Cubs by the time they returned home.

The Terrymen won nine of 11 games against the western clubs to move into first place with a one-game lead over the Cubs. The successful stand represented the 1937 Giants at their best. Ott led the attack, clouting six home runs and hitting safely in each of the 11 games. The rest of the team, particularly Ripple, hit well, and Bartell and Whitehead continued their brilliant play in the field. McCarthy was sensational at first base, and Ott, while hardly a polished third baseman, was playing a sound, dependable game at the bag. And all of the regular starters except Hubbell, of all people, won against the Western teams, although King Carl did save a victory for Melton over the Reds.

Amidst all the excitement during the home stand, it was rumored that Alva Bradley, owner of the Cleveland Indians, had made Terry an attractive offer to replace Steve O'Neill as manager. This was flatly denied by Bradley, but there was a strong feeling that an offer had been made and that Terry was considering it seriously. Finally, on September 7, Stoneham ended all speculation by signing Terry to a five-year contract as general manager. Stoneham explained, "We felt it was much better to take this action now and end all of the rumors rather than wait until the end of the season. Bill will continue as manager, and he also will be responsible for directing our farm system, making deals, and signing players." The last-named duty was greeted with little enthusiasm by several of the players, especially Leiber, Danning, and Bartell, who had experienced difficulties in negotiating contracts with the tough-bargaining Terry.

The Giants headed west for the last time, with a 1½-game lead which they increased to a 2½-game edge before they arrived in Chicago for the final three-game set. Charlie Root won the first game, but Melton evened the series with a sparkling shutout. Schumacher started against Curt Davis in the pivotal third game before a large midweek crowd.

The Polo Grounders held a 3 to 0 lead after three innings, but the Cubs knocked out Schumacher and tied the game off Hubbell, who relieved Prince Hal. The Giants moved ahead 8 to 3, but the Cubs drove out Hubbell and Harry Gumbert came in and held them off with the score 8 to

6. Gumbert lasted until the bottom of the ninth when the Cubs loaded the bases with one out. Terry, sparing none of his horses, waved in Melton, who retired Carl Reynolds on a fly ball for the second out as a run scored to cut the lead to 8 to 7. With the winning run on base, Augie Galan stepped up. The fleet outfielder worked Melton to a full count and then tapped a slow bouncer to the right of the straining Melton. Ott raced in, shouted Melton off the ball, and gunned out Galan to end the game. The Giants returned home triumphantly with a 3½-game lead over Chicago.

Terry's club kept up the pace after returning to the Polo Grounds, taking four in a row from the Dodgers and the Bees as the pitching staff got some much-needed help from two new members, Walter (Jumbo) Brown and Bill Lohrman. Then, on September 30, in Philadelphia, the Giants clinched the pennant on Hubbell's 2 to 1 win over righthander Claude Passeau. It was a classic 1937 Giant win—Hubbell's airtight pitching, good defense, and a one-run victory.

Coach Pancho Snyder managed the team in the clincher with Terry back in New York nursing a heavy cold. In their clubhouse the Giants were their usual undemonstrative selves except for the ebullient Bartell. The little shortstop held up the ball he had caught for the final out and loudly proclaimed, ''Now bring on those Yanks.''

Hubbell had another brilliant year, leading the league with 22 wins and 159 strikeouts and extending his epic winning streak to 24. Melton had an outstanding rookie season with 20 wins, ranking second in the league in saves and earned-run-average, and fourth in strikeouts. Bartell and Whitehead held the infield together again with their adroit, steady play, and Bartell's consistent hitting in the early months kept the offense going when Ott was laboring through his long slump. Ott, who had come back to have a great second half, tied Joe Medwick for the home run lead with 31, led the league in walks, and finished fifth in RBI's. Most experts considered the successful switch of Ott to third base, which permittted the potent Ripple to play regularly, and Melton's strong season as the keys to the Giants' pennant win.

The odds again heavily favored the Yankees as the teams prepared for the World Series. After all, the Bronx Bombers had beaten the Giants decisively the previous fall and had dominated the American League a second time, while the Giants again had to struggle to win the pennant. Still, there were some who thought the Giants had a better chance than in 1936. DiMaggio, Gehrig, and Dickey were as devastating as in 1936, but the other Yanks—Lazzeri, Rolfe, Crosetti, Powell, Selkirk—had fallen back. Moreover, the Giants had a much more balanced pitching staff than in 1936 when they were almost completely dependent on Hubbell. This time the general feeling was that even if Hubbell should fail it would not necessarily finish off the Terrymen.

The opener was played at Yankee Stadium before 60,573, with Gomez opposing Hubbell. Behind 1 to 0 in the six inning, the Yanks came back with a vengeance when Gomez walked and moved to second on Crosetti's hit. With Rolfe up, Mancuso whipped a bullseye peg down to second that appeared to have picked off Gomez. But Bartell dropped the throw as Lefty dove back to the bag. Rolfe then singled to load the bases, and DiMaggio laced a single to center for the first two runs. Dickey brought in the third run with an infield hit, and Selkirk drove in two more with a solid hit to right. That was enough for Terry. He took out Hubbell and motioned in Dick Coffman.

As Coffman began the long walk in from the bullpen, the perplexing announcement boomed out over the loudspeaker, "Gumbert, Number 10, now pitching for the Giants." This astonished the crowd as Harry Gumbert was sitting quietly in the Giant dugout, hardly ready to face the murderous Yankees. As it turned out, the mistake was not the announcer's but rather that of Captain Gus Mancuso, who had notified Plate Umpire Red Ormsby erroneously that Gumbert was the reliever. The rules required Gumbert to pitch to at least one batter so the cold righthander rose resignedly from the bench, peeled off his jacket, and replaced the warmed-up Coffman on the mound. Gumbert took his allotted eight warm-up throws, added a few extra tosses to first base for good measure, then bent to the task of retiring Lazzeri. He did his job as Tony bounced to Whitehead, but Burgess let the ball roll through his legs for an error and the Yanks had their sixth run. Coffman hastily took the mound but allowed another run before retiring the side.

That was the story of the game as Gomez won easily, his fourth World Series victory without a loss. After the game Terry, ignoring the shellacking absorbed by Hubbell, said, "That throw that Bartell dropped with Gomez six feet off the bag was the break of the game."

In the second game it was Red Ruffing against Melton before 57,675. The game was almost a carbon copy of the opener. The Giants scored in the first inning when Ott drove in Bartell. Helped along by Bartell's defensive heroics, Melton held the Yanks scoreless until the fifth when Selkirk drove in Myril Hoag,. Two more hits brought in Selkirk and prompted the removal of Melton, who was replaced by Gumbert. This time Harry's entrance was made uneventfully, and he succeeded in retiring the Yanks and holding the score to 2 to 1. But the Bronx Bombers moved well ahead in the sixth and went on to win 8 to 1 as Ruffing polished off the Giants effortlessly.

"What is there to say?" croaked Terry hoarsely, still feeling the effects of the heavy cold which had plagued him since the Giants clinched the pennant. "Those guys just beat the hell out of us." Fans and writers recalled that the Yankees had crushed their National League opponents in four straight in the 1927, 1928, and 1932 World Series, and there was considerable speculation that the machine-like Yanks were headed for another grand slam Series victory. With this a looming possibility, the classic moved across the Harlem River to the Polo Grounds.

In the third game it was Pearson against Schumacher before 37,395. Danning started the game in place of Mancuso when it was discovered that Gus had a broken finger on his throwing hand. It was the same melancholy story as the Giants lost 5 to 1. The Yanks chopped away methodically at Schumacher, scoring single runs in the second, fourth, and fifth innings and two runs in the third. The Giants were helpless offensively. After the game Terry said grimly, "Who would have thought that we would have been held to only three runs so far in three games?" Unaware that McCarthy had announced that Bump Hadley would pitch the following day, Terry added, "I'll be surprised if they don't start Gomez tomorrow. Hub will pitch for us."

A Saturday afternoon crowd of 44,293 was on hand for the fourth game, fully expecting that it would be the last game of the Series. For some reason the Yanks were annoyed at Terry's offhand prediction that Gomez would start. Apparently they considered it an affront to Hadley. As a result, the usual needling between the teams had a special edge from the start of the game.

The Yanks scored in the first inning when Rolfe tripled and DiMaggio drove him in. The Giants fought back to tie the game and then shot ahead 6 to 1 after two innings on hits by Moore, Bartell, and Leiber.

As the game continued, the jockeying between the clubs intensified. The Giants became particulary incensed at some of Art Fletcher's antics in the third base coaching box. The lantern-jawed Fletcher was noted for his ability to steal signs and pick up telltale mannerisms of opposing players. Fletcher tried to stir up Hubbell by going through motions indicating he was stealing signs and tipping off the hitters. At one point the normally easy-going Ott became so infuriated that he called time and went to the mound. He begged his roommate and bosom pal, "Come on, Hub, dust a couple of them off just to shut Fletcher up." "What for?" replied the unruffled Hubbell. "He's trying to get your goat by making you think he's stealing our signs," answered Ott. The great lefthander shrugged and responded, "Don't worry, Mel. Fletcher's not fooling anyone. He isn't bothering me at all, and besides I'm not going to start throwing dusters at this stage of the game."

Hubbell continued to handle the dynamic Yanks with ease, yielding only a harmless bases-empty home run to Gehrig in the ninth. The final score was 7 to 3 and the Giants' redoubtable "meal ticket" had at least averted another Yankee sweep. After the game the Yankees were snappish despite their still-imposing position in the Series. "So Terry was surprised that I didn't pitch Gomez today, eh?" growled McCarthy. "Well, let him run his club and I'll run mine!" The belligerent Fletcher added, "Terry's the guy that's down. Let him crawl out of it."

And so the Series moved into its fifth game, with Gomez facing Melton before 38,216 fans. The Yankees took a one-run lead in the second inning when Hoag lofted an outside fastball into the right field seats. DiMaggio increased the lead to 2 to 0 in the top of the third with a tremendous blast that cleared the top of the left field stands and banged into one of the flagpoles arising from the Polo Grounds roof. The Giants fought their way back in the bottom of the third as Bartell singled, and the overdue Ott, held to three singles in the first four games, tied the game with a clout deep into the upper right field stands. In the fifth, Lazzeri opened with a triple and scored on Gomez's infield hit. Lefty scored the final Yankee run on Gehrig's double.

Gomez's performance was distinguished not only by his pitching mastery and his rare base hit but also for his nonchalance on the mound. In one of the late innings, with a Giant runner on first and the dangerous Ott at bat, Gomez stepped off the mound to stare up at a passing plane. The crowd buzzed in amusement while Joe McCarthy fidgeted uneasily in the dugout. After the plane moved out of sight, the casual Gomez stepped back on the mound and proceeded to rub the Giants out easily on the way to a 4 to 2 win and another Yankee Series victory.

McCarthy and Fletcher were jubilant in the clubhouse. Fletcher told the writers, "Why don't you guys go back and tell Terry—well, what the hell," he interrupted himself in midsentence. "He's all right, everything's all right. Just tell Terry that I hope he gets over his cold soon and that we meet him and his gang in the Series again next year." The acrimony of the day before had disappeared with the Yankee triumph.

Interviewed after the game, Terry at first complained uncharacteristically about the umpiring in the Series. But after a while the man from Memphis gained his equanimity and talked candidly about the Series, his disappointment, and his admiration for the Yankees. After all, the Giants had been beaten soundly and, as the *World-Telegraph's* Joe Williams put it, "The turning point of the Series was when the Yanks suited up for the first game."

8

The Ranks Are Decimated

After training for the 1938 season at Baton Rouge, Louisiana, and completing their annual barnstorming tour with the Indians, the Giants were ready to go after their third straight pennant. McCarthy was set at first base, with Sam Leslie in reserve. Chiozza replaced Whitehead, who was out for the season following a nervous breakdown. Bartell was primed for another good year, and Ott was playing third base with more assurance after a full preseason at third. Blondy Ryan and Mickey Haslin, a journeyman infielder formerly with Boston and Philadelphia, were the utility infielders.

Ripple started the season in right, with Leiber in center, Moore in left, and Wally Berger in reserve. Harry Danning had won the starting catcher's slot from Mancuso because of his heavier hitting. The pitching staff looked solid enough with Hubbell, Melton, Schumacher, and Gumbert in the starting rotation and Castleman scheduled to join them after he recuperated from back surgery. Two young righthanders, Bill Lohrman and Hy Vandenberg, showed promise, and Dick Coffman and Jumbo Brown were the relief pitchers.

Favored to win again, the Giants started off beautifully, winning 18 of their first 21 games to take a five-game lead over the second-place Cubs. John Drebinger of the *Times* described their start as "one of the most impressive breaks from the barrier a serious pennant contender has been able to effect in years." The only problem in sight was second base with Whitehead gone and Chiozza, his replacement, not hitting.

By Memorial Day the Giants remained in first place, 2½ games ahead of the Cubs. With neither Chiozza or Mickey Haslin adequate at second base, Terry traded Wally Berger to the Reds for second baseman Alex Kampouris. The Giants replaced Berger by purchasing outfielder Bob Seeds from Newark, where he had been burning up the International

League. There were other changes as Terry maneuvered to keep his club on top. An injury to Jo-Jo Moore forced Ott's return to the outfield with Blondy Ryan going to third. And Sam Leslie replaced the slumping McCarthy at first for a number of games. Despite these difficulties, the Giants held their own through June and on July 4 led the league, 3½ games ahead of the Pirates and six games up on the Cubs.

The Dodgers were of special interest, not only because of the traditional Giant-Dodger rivalry but also because this was dynamic Larry MacPhail's first year running the club. MacPhail had shaken up the Giant and Yankee front offices by unilaterally going the night game route in 1938, and later on in the year he scrapped a long-standing agreement between the three clubs by announcing plans to broadcast Dodger games in 1939.

The Giants were represented on the All-Star squad by Hubbell, Ott, Moore, Leiber, Danning, and Terry, who managed the National League team. Memphis Bill had the satisfaction of seeing the National League regain some of its lost prestige as it defeated the American Leaguers at Cincinnati's Crosley Field 4 to 1. Ott played the entire game in center field and whacked a triple, the longest hit of the day. Hank Leiber, who pinch-hit, was the only other Giant to play.

The Giants slipped after the midseason break and relinquished first place to the Pirates just before arriving in Chicago to complete their third western tour. Gabby Hartnett was named to replace Charley Grimm as manager the day before the Giants arrived, and a capacity crowd watched Bill Lee and Dizzy Dean win the first two games.

Dean had been sidelined with a sore arm most of the time since joining the Cubs just before Opening Day. The Great One showed no sign of his one-time speed but exhibited a remarkable display of sheer pitching wizardry as he kept the Giant hitters off balance all through the game. While waiting in vain for that famed high, hard one that Dean used to "fog thoo," the Terry forces fished futilely for a sweeping sidearm curve and a tantalizing mini-screwball. Dean's victory was enlivened by a violent brawl between Bartell and Billy Jurges. It started when Jurges crashed hard into Bartell at second on a rundown play. The two shortstops rolled around the bag kicking and punching, and it took a number of the players to pry them apart. As the Giants returned to their dugout, Jimmy Ripple commented, "Well, the season is official now—Bartell finally got into a scrap."

The disastrous road trip ended the next day when Hubbell, in relief of Lohrman and Gumbert, lost a 15-inning game to Bill Lee. The Giants returned home four games behind the Pirates having won only four of 13 decisions on the trip.

Things continued to deteriorate after the Giants returned home. Chiozza broke his collarbone and was finished for the season. Schumacher developed bone chips in his pitching arm which hampered him for the rest of the season and required postseason surgery. Kampouris was a flop, and Bill Cissell was purchased from Baltimore and inserted at second base.

The final blow came on August 18 when Hubbell sustained a serious elbow injury while pitching against the Dodgers. After the game, he said ruefully, "My elbow felt as though knives were cutting through it every time I tried to put anything on the ball." Hub continued, "I've had some pains going back to 1934, but they always worked themselves out before long. But I'm afraid this is a different story." A few days later Hubbell had a bone chip removed and was finished for the year.

Ott, who was carrying the club offensively, received a fine tribute from Pirate manager Pie Traynor. Pie told Garry Schumacher of the *Journal-American*, "You newspaper fellows write a great deal about ballplayers and love to compare them. But when you talk about National League players, Ottie has got to be the best in all the years I've been with the Pirates. My logic is simple. The best players are those who win the most games, and I can't name a player who has exerted as strong an influence upon so many games as Mel. I know that he personally has beaten the Pirates more often than any other player, and on the other teams the players I talk to express the same thought."

A short time after this professional testimonial to his ability, Ott received tangible evidence of his personal appeal to the fans. A cereal company ran a contest to determine the most popular major league player at each position. Master Mel received the most votes of all the third basemen, and the rightfielders as well, and was rewarded with a resplendent, robins-egg blue sedan.

Considering their injuries, the Giants did well to finish in third place, clinching that spot on the last day of the season when Gumbert beat Boston. Individually, only Ott, Danning, and Moore had good years. Ott led the league in homers with 36 and in runs scored, was second in runs-batted-in and walks, and third in total bases. Defensively, his willingness and ability to shift back and forth between right field and third base gave Terry at least some of the defensive flexibility he needed. Danning, despite personal difficulties with Terry, established himself solidly as the regular catcher with his solid hitting and improved handling of pitchers. Moore, although handicapped by injuries, hit .302.

Meanwhile the Cubs, after falling well behind the Pirates, fought back in a manner highly reminiscent of their great 1935 stretch drive. Hartnett and Rip Collins led the hitting attack and Clay Bryant and Bill Lee pitched superbly as the Cubs won 20 of 23 games to pull even with Traynor's club. The Cubs moved ahead on Hartnett's dramatic, tie-breaking homer in the ninth inning off Mace Brown in the gathering darkness of Wrigley Field and went on to clinch the pennant three days later leaving the Pirates with broken dreams of their first title since 1925 (and thousands of unusable World Series tickets).

None of the Giants or their fans were surprised by the outcome of the World Series after the Giants' experience with the Yanks in 1936 and 1937. The Bronx Bombers polished off the Cubs in four straight.

There was considerable speculation among Giant fans as to the moves that would be made to revitalize the club. Terry and Stoneham responded first by completing a major trade in early December with the Cubs. Bartell, Leiber, and Mancuso were traded for their opposite numbers on the Cubs: shortstop Billy Jurges, outfielder Frank Demaree, and catcher Ken O'Dea. After the deal was announced, a writer asked Terry, "What do you think of the trade?" Never one to suffer fools or foolish questions gladly, Terry snapped, "What the hell do *you* think I think of it? I just made the trade!"

The following week the Giants obtained first baseman Henry (Zeke) Bonura from the Washington Senators. The Giants gave up pitcher Tom Baker, who had shown little since he was obtained from the Dodgers, a young minor league first baseman, Jim Carlin, and $25,000. A New Orleans native, the powerful Bonura had been one of the American League's hardest hitters in four years with the Chicago White Sox and in 1938 with the Senators. His fielding was another matter.

One of the Washington writers, having observed Bonura's still-life, wooden Indian style at first base for a full season, commented, "I hope Mel Ott hasn't signed yet. The extra chasing he'll be doing in right field in back of Zeke ought to be worth at least a few extra thousand dollars." Despite this, Terry was pleased at bolstering the Giants' attack. "I know all about Zeke's fielding," he said, "but we're prepared to work on that. What counts most is that we've finally got a first baseman who can powder the ball."

There had been rumors that Memphis Bill was tiring of his dual role as field manager and overseer of the Giant farm system and that he wanted to relinquish the field role. Several writers speculated that Stoneham might be interested in bringing Frankie Frisch into the Giant organization as the field manager. Frisch had been let out as manager by the Cardinals just before the season ended. But Stoneham supported Terry handsomely, commenting, "If we owned 15 farm clubs, Bill Terry would still remain manager of the Giants. He's the best manager in baseball. When the need comes for someone to direct the farm clubs exclusively, we'll get someone else."

Larry MacPhail, having opened up the New York City area to night baseball, announced that the Dodgers planned to broadcast all of their home and away games beginning in 1939. In January the Yanks and Giants, bowing to the inevitable, made arrangements to broadcast all home games except Sunday games over Station WABC. Mel Allen handled the early broadcasts along with Arch McDonald.

There were a number of question marks as the Giants regrouped in spring training. Hubbell, Schumacher, and Castleman were recuperating from surgery and their progress was watched closely. Among the other pitchers in camp were Gumbert, Melton, Lohrman, Johnny Wittig, Dick Coffman, Jumbo Brown, Manuel Salvo, and Hy Vandenberg.

Danning, with Mancuso gone, began a season for the first time as the uncontested first-string catcher. Ken O'Dea and Tommy Padden were the backup receivers.

The infield was unsettled except for shortstop where Jurges was unchallenged. Bonura, of course, had to be considered the regular first baseman although McCarthy was still on hand. Second base presented an unclear picture with Whitehead having missed the entire 1938 season and Chiozza, Kampouris, Bill Cissell, and Alban Glossop, obtained from the Reds, waiting in the wings. At third base two youngsters, George Myatt and Tom Hafey, up from the Giants' Knoxville affiliate, competed for the starting job.

The regular outfield appeared set with Ott (newly installed as captain) back in right field, Frank Demaree in center, and Moore in left. Jimmy Ripple and Bob Seeds backed up the starting trio.

Bonura, a good-natured, outgoing fellow, became an immediate favorite among the writers. He was a made-to-order source of good copy with his valiant struggle to attain respectability in the field, his murderous hitting, and his uninhibited exuberance. His first meeting with the youthful Stoneham was the talk of the camp. On being introduced to his new boss, who was visiting the team during a game with the Indians in Zeke's native New Orleans, Bonura responded with a blithe, "Say, Horace, for a club owner you're a mighty fine-looking young fellow. You ought to be playing ball yourself. By the way, how about coming out to my house for one of my mother's famous Italian dishes?"

Picked to finish second behind Cincinnati, the Giants had their poorest start since Terry took over the club. The first New York World's Fair had just opened, and Terry, Hubbell, and Ott participated in a baseball clinic at the Fair. At that time the Giants were in seventh place while the Dodgers, now managed by Leo Durocher, roosted in second place. Terry found himself surrounded by young hecklers from Brooklyn. A group of them shouted a number of pointed questions at the Giant manager, questions like, "Is Brooklyn still in the league?" and "Do you think you'll make it out of the second division?" Terry brought a round of appreciative laughter with the sly response, "I realize the Giants are only in seventh and the Dodgers in second. But I'm sure Durocher and his gang feel just as much out of place as we do."

After splitting a Memorial Day double-header with the Dodgers, the Giants were in fifth place, half a game behind Durocher's club. The pitching was mediocre and only Gumbert and Lohrman were pitching well. Hubbell, Schumacher, and Castleman were having post-surgery problems, and Melton and Salvo were completely ineffective. The only bright spots were the hitting of Bonura, Ott, and Danning and the effective defensive play of Whitehead and Jurges.

Bonura had become a big Polo Grounds favorite despite his atrocious fielding. The fans loved to watch big Zeke hit, and they were intrigued by some of his fielding mannerisms as well, particularly his manner of handling unassisted putouts. After snaring a ground ball Bonura would charge to the bag with his right arm outstretched and his palm down, looking for all the world like Bronco Nagurski straight-arming a would-be tackler.

There was a memorable team hitting performance against Cincinnati at the Polo Grounds on June 6 when the Giants broke the major league record for home runs in one inning by hitting five (Danning, Demaree, Whitehead, Salvo, and Moore) and tied the record of seven for a game.

By early July, the Giants had moved up to second place, four games behind the Reds, after a tempestuous double-header with the Dodgers at the Polo Grounds on July 2. Leo Durocher's club won the opener 3 to 2 before more than 51,000 highly excited fans by routing Bill Lohrman and weathering a Giant threat in the eighth on Ott's two-run homer off Luke Hamlin.

With Schumacher facing Whitlow Wyatt in the second game, the Giants moved out to an early 4 to 0 lead. The Dodgers came back in the fourth with three runs, driving out Schumacher. Durocher ended the inning by banging into a double play. As Lippy Leo crossed the bag and ran down the baseline there was an astonishing sight. Bonura, after taking the third out throw, wheeled and chased Durocher. On the way Zeke fired the ball at Leo's head, barely missing, and then threw his glove at Durocher. Bonura closed in on the Dodger manager and with his left arm clamped a hammerlock around Leo's head, meanwhile delivering a series of uppercuts. Durocher returned fire with an assortment of body blows.

For a moment it looked as if the fight would extend to other players as both dugouts emptied onto the field. But the umpires managed to avert a free-for-all and the two belligerents were separated and ejected. As Bonura and Durocher marched their separate ways to the clubhouse the cheers and jeers were about equally divided. The fans showered the field with pop bottles and assorted fruits and vegetables.

After the Dodgers tied the game at 4-all, Danning broke the tie in the eighth with a homer and the Giants won 6 to 4. The large crowd left, still tingling with excitement over the fight and the two tight games.

Later in the Giant clubhouse Bonura was still furious. The writers were curious as to what had happened since the fight had flared up so suddenly and unexpectedly. "That little bastard spiked me deliberately," Zeke fumed. "You know I don't ask for trouble but I'm not going to take that from anyone." Durocher's only comment was, "If that big clown hadn't got his foot in the way, I wouldn't have been close to him." Actually, Leo felt that Schumacher had been throwing at the Dodgers and, with Hal out of the game, Bonura became the fall guy for Leo's retaliation.

The Giants played the Dodgers at Ebbets Field less than a week after the Polo Grounds incident. With feelings running high, 25 additional police were detailed to cover the game. The possibility of trouble was further enhanced when Durocher discovered a published statement, attributed to Bonura, to the effect that Zeke had said three Dodgers told him that he should have "punched the daylights" out of Durocher for the Polo Grounds spiking.

"My men haven't lied to me yet," barked Durocher before the game. "I don't think they're lying now when they tell me none of 'em said any such thing to Bonura or anybody else. Dolph Camilli told me he would take a sock at anybody who charged him with making such a statement." MacPhail considered bringing the affair to a showdown by calling all the Dodgers in front of Bonura, but he decided against it.

After all the anticipation of further hostilities nothing unusual happened. The first game was a typically tense Giant-Dodger affair which the Dodgers won 3 to 2 with Wyatt outpitching Melton. The next day the two rivals split a double-header again, with none of the fireworks that occurred at the Polo Grounds. The teams moved into the All-Star game break with the Reds in first place, ahead of the second-place Giants by 5½ games and in front of the Dodgers, Cubs, and Cardinals by eight games.

Ott, Jurges, and Danning were voted to the National League All-Star squad, which lost 3 to 1 at Yankee Stadium. Ott, the only Giant participant, played the entire game in center field and contributed two hits.

The resurgent Giants began the second half of the season by taking on the western teams at the Polo Grounds. They split the first two games of a three-game set with the Reds, as Schumacher's loss to Bucky Walters was offset by Lohrman's win over Paul Derringer.

The third game would be remembered for many years to come. Harry Gumbert held a 4 to 3 lead over Gene Thompson as the Reds came to bat in the eighth inning. With a runner on in the top of the inning, Harry Craft lined a low, curving drive into the lower left field stands at the foul pole. Plate umpire Lee Ballanfant ruled it a fair ball, pulling the Reds into a 5 to 4 lead. Danning stormed around Ballanfant, shoving the official and shouting his protest of the call. After a few minutes Ballanfant's patience was exhausted, and Harry the Horse was thumbed out of the game.

But the protest was still building. The Giants took their case to Ziggy Sears, who was umpiring at second. After a long harangue with Sears, the easy-going Jo-Jo Moore, who presumably had the best view of the ball when it passed the foul pole, was thrown out of the game. The Giants still had plenty of manpower left, and they continued the verbal assault until big George Magerkurth, the first base umpire, moved up to home plate to try to terminate the argument. As he moved toward the center of the debate he began to talk animatedly with Billy Jurges. Suddenly, according to Magerkurth's account, Jurges shouted at him, "Don't you spit in my face." Magerkurth, his face reddening, bellowed back, "Don't get your

71

face so near mine and it won't get spit on." Jurges roared, "I'll spit on yours." The Major responded, "I'd like to see you do that." Billy obliged. With that, Magerkurth belted Jurges in the ribs, and Billy responded with a punch to the umpire's cheek.

The fisticuffs brought the protest to an abrupt halt as Ballanfant ordered Jurges off the field. The Giants, suddenly realizing the seriousness of the situation, joined in pushing their blazing shortstop in the direction of the clubhouse. It was a patchwork lineup that the Giants had left after the stormy 15-minute interruption. Chiozza was moved from third to short. Ott came in to play third. With Ripple already used as a pinch-hitter and out of the game, Johnny McCarthy went to right field and Hal Schumacher took over center field. The Giants lost the game 8 to 4.

(The incident is of special interest to the baseball historian because it resulted in the installation of a net along the length of each Polo Grounds foul pole to aid umpires in determining whether balls hit close to the poles were fair or foul. Many of today's ball parks are similarly equipped.)

The next day Ford Frick announced immediate 10-day suspensions for both Jurges and Magerkurth and fines of $150. Danning, Moore, and Terry were fined $50 each, Terry's fine "for failing to cooperate in handling the situation." The Giants took the field against the Cardinals with Chiozza at shortstop and Ott at third. To add to their problems, Danning reported with a leg infection and was hospitalized. With the Giants losing 4 to 3 in the top of the ninth, Cardinal pitcher Clyde Shoun lifted a fly into short left. Chiozza, inexperienced at short, and Moore both raced for it. Lou caught it just before Jo-Jo crashed into him with terrific force.

Both players were knocked sprawling, writhing in pain in the outfield grass as the players of both teams raced to their assistance. Moore was helped to his feet in a few minutes and was able to walk around and continue in the game. But Chiozza suffered a compound fracture of the leg and was taken off the field on a stretcher moaning in pain. He was finished for the season.

Burgess Whitehead moved over to short, and Kampouris came in to play second. But the Giants lost, falling seven games behind the Reds. Hubbell lost to the Cards the next day, and the Giants slid another full game behind the Reds.

Next the Giants lost three straight to the Pirates, the third loss coming when Chuck Klein hit a three-run homer in the ninth off Melton to overcome a 3 to 1 Giant lead. During this series Jumbo Brown was hit by an Arky Vaughan liner and joined Chiozza and Danning on the hospital list. The Giants had lost seven games in a row and were in fifth place, 10 games out of first.

With the Giants' season crumbling before their eyes, Stoneham appealed to Frick to permit Jurges to return to action. But his appeal was turned down. In desperation Terry recalled Tom Hafey from Jersey City and picked up tiny Frank Scalzi, a free agent, to play shortstop. Scalzi had played in the Cleveland Indian farm system but had never appeared in a major league game.

The Giants lost the last two games of the home stand to the Cubs to fall ignominiously to sixth place, 12½ games behind the Reds. They lost the first game 8 to 7 as the jittery Scalzi committed four errors. Gumbert, pitching in relief in the last game, lost a two-run lead in the ninth inning. The team had won one, then lost nine in a row to close out the most disastrous home stand in the memory of most Giant fans.

A few weeks later the Giants made one more attempt to move back into the first division, taking a double-header from Manager Casey Stengel's Boston Bees to move into a virtual tie with the Pirates for fourth place. The second game exhibited Stengel's comic talent at its best.

With the score tied at 5-all after 10 innings, darkness began to set in over the Polo Grounds, which had not yet been equipped with lights. The umpires agreed to play either one more full inning or to eight o'clock (whichever came first). Hubbell, who had regained some of his old form, retired the Bees quickly in the top of the eleventh. In the bottom of the inning, Demaree opened with a walk. The infield crept in to pounce upon Ott's certain sacrifice bunt. But Master Mel reached out and cracked a double to left which practically decapitated onrushing third baseman Hank Majeski. Danning was walked intentionally.

With the moon preparing to peek over Coogan's Bluff, the ebullient Stengel waved in pitcher Freddy Frankhouse from the bullpen with a flashlight. Casey kept bellowing ''What time is it?'' to the umpires after each pitch, with the clock over the center-field clubhouse swallowed in darkness. But it was still just a quarter of eight whether Casey knew it or not. Frankhouse's second pitch to Bonura sailed back to the screen as Demaree trotted across with the winning run, and the disconsolate Stengel began the long walk to the distant clubhouse.

On August 13th, the Giants had another seven home run game, this time against the Phils. This duplicated their earlier feat against the Reds as Demaree hit two homers and Bonura, Kampouris, Moore, Seeds, and Bill Lohrman hit one apiece. Since the Giants' first record-breaking performance, the Yankees had extended the record to eight home runs in a game against the Philadelphia Athletics.

On Labor Day the Giants were in fourth place, half a game ahead of the Dodgers but 13 games behind the league-leading Reds. A few days later, during a series with the Dodgers, there was a bizarre affair involving Whitehead. The high-strung second baseman had gone through a poor season, compounded by the team's misfortunes in July. In mid-August he was suspended indefinitely for what Terry described as ''infraction of club rules.'' It developed that Whitey had shown up just a few minutes before game time for a game with the Dodgers. The following day he was not at Ebbets Field for the game. This led directly to his suspension. Whitehead, it turned out, had appeared instead at the Yankee Stadium in full uniform and sought permission to work out with the Yanks. Joe McCarthy, of course, vetoed the idea. Two days later Whitehead rejoined the Giants. The club had decided to rescind the suspension although Whitehead hardly was back in Terry's good graces. In mid-September Burgess left the team again and this time was suspended for the rest of the season.

Despite Bonura's .321 average, Terry had lost all patience with Zeke because of his fielding weaknesses. Memphis Bill became so disenchanted that he indicated publicly that Bonura would not be his first baseman in 1940. Babe Young, in the Giant farm system since 1936, was brought up from Knoxville to determine if he was ready to play regularly. He played the rest of the season and impressed everyone with his relaxed lefthand pull-hitting style and effective play at first base. In other moves Terry released Dick Coffman, sold Jimmy Ripple to the Dodgers, and purchased a young, highly regarded outfielder, Johnny Rucker, from the Atlanta club.

As the season wound down, the Giants sank unhappily into fifth place, finishing 18½ games behind the Reds and a humiliating six games behind the third-place Dodgers. Only Hubbell, Gumbert, and Ott were among the leaders in any of the statistical categories. Hubbell was second in earned-run-average, and Gumbert was fourth in the league in winning percentage with 18 wins and 11 losses. Ott, despite missing the last month of play with severe charleyhorses, was second in home runs, only one behind Johnny Mize, and second to Dolph Camilli in bases on balls.

There were the usual rumors that Terry would be replaced as manager. Frankie Frisch's name bobbed up again as the most likely successor. Again Stoneham reaffirmed his confidence in Terry and announced that Memphis Bill would continue to manage the Giants in 1940.

9

The Doldrums

Through the fall of 1939 Stoneham and Terry pondered their next moves. The club had slipped from first to third in 1938, now it had finished in fifth place. Attendance was down. To complicate matters the Giants' downfall was accompanied by the rise of the Dodgers, who had climbed to third under the aggressive leadership of MacPhail and Durocher. New York fans other than the Flatbush Faithful began to realize that the Giants were no longer the only National League club in New York.

Stoneham and Terry considered the Giant farm system the most logical means of revitalizing the team—unlike MacPhail who picked up and discarded players like so many chewing gum wrappers. When Terry took over the club in 1932 the Giants had only 27 players in their organization, all of them on the Giant roster. By midseason of 1939 the Giants owned or controlled the contracts of well over 100 players. This included 82 minor league players either directly owned by the Giants or on teams with which the Giants had a working agreement. The club owned franchises in Jersey City; Clinton, Iowa; and Fort Smith, Arkansas, and had working agreements with clubs in Milford, Delaware; Salisbury, Maryland; Amarillo (operated by outfielder Bob Seeds' wife); Knoxville; and Nashville. With the farm system growing, Terry finally convinced Stoneham that its supervision was a fulltime job. In December Jack Cook, the secretary of the Jersey City team, was given that assignment.

The farm system talent was not yet ready for the majors, so the Giants were forced to buy promising minor league players. They had purchased Johnny Rucker from Atlanta before the 1939 season ended. In December, infielder Mickey Witek was acquired from the Yankees' prime breeding franchise at Newark. The Giants parted with Alex Kampouris, catcher Tommy Padden, and $40,000 for Witek, who had been named the most valuable player in the International League for 1939.

The team that began training at Winter Haven was loaded with question marks. The catching appeared to be solid enough with Danning at his peak and Ken O'Dea backing up Harry. But the pitching staff was something else. Gumbert was now the leading starter. Hubbell and Schumacher clearly could no longer be expected to equal their heroics of past years. Melton had gone through two mediocre seasons after his outstanding rookie year in 1937. Lohrman and Vandenberg had yet to perform up to their early promise, and Manuel Salvo had also been a disappointment. Lefty Roy Joiner, brought up from Jersey City, was an unknown quantity. He joined Jumbo Brown and Jim Lynn as a reliever. Righthanders Bob Carpenter and Johnny Wittig were on hand. Castleman was in camp only a few weeks before it became apparent that his back miseries would not permit him to continue, and Slick was put on the voluntarily retired list. The Giants also had picked up sore-armed Paul Dean over the winter as a free agent.

The infield had potential, but the only settled position was at shortstop with the accomplished Jurges. Babe Young appeared ready to replace the disqualified Bonura. Witek showed promise at second base. Whitehead, more or less back in the manager's good graces, had been shifted to third.

In the outfield Demaree was a sound player, but Moore had slowed down perceptibly and Ott had a terrible spring, hitting infrequently and with little of his customary power. Most of the attention was focused on handsome Johnny Rucker, who became the camp sensation after a few unsteady weeks, gaining almost instant celebrity when Life magazine published a feature story on his life and times as an up-and-coming rookie in his first spring training camp.

Bonura, protesting a big cut in his $15,000 salary, reported unsigned at Stoneham's request. He was permitted to stay in camp at the club's expense, much to the disgust of Terry who never coddled signed regulars much less an unsigned ex-regular who no longer fit in his plans. Zeke was given permission to make a deal for himself. Eventually, he was traded back to the Senators for $10,000 and a year's option on the services of a young lefthander, Rene Monteagudo, who did not pan out.

For the first time since 1933, Terry's first full year as manager, the pollsters forecast a second division finish for the Giants. Despite these predictions, the club started off surprisingly well as Danning and Young hit with power, Jurges and Whitehead steadied the infield, and Gumbert, Hubbell, Melton, and Lohrman pitched well.

During the winter Stoneham and Terry had decided to equip the Polo Grounds for night baseball, and $125,000 worth of lights and auxiliary equipment were installed. The Giants' first night game ever at the Polo Grounds on May 24 was a big success as Gumbert took an 8 to 1 decision from Casey Stengel's inept Bees.

The Terrymen had a big Memorial Day. They won a doubleheader from the Dodgers at Ebbets Field and in the bargain knocked Durocher's club out of the lead. Hubbell pitched a masterpiece in the first game as he held the Dodgers to one hit and faced only 27 batters. Johnny Hudson got the Dodger hit in the third inning, but he was promptly erased in a double play. No other Dodger reached base. The Giants wound up the day in third place, only four games behind the first-place Reds and two behind the Dodgers.

In early June Terry replaced the slumping Ott in the cleanup spot with Babe Young. This was the first time since Ott became a regular in 1928 that he was not batting cleanup. In another surprise Ott showed up before a game wearing glasses. As Mel explained it, "I suppose I've always been nearsighted, but it's only been the last few years that I've noticed it, and particularly over this season. I'll tell you one thing," he grinned. "Before this it was tough in the outfield, too. If something stayed up in the sky I knew it was a bird, but if it came down it was a fly ball."

On June 23 the Giants suffered a crippling blow. Billy Jurges came to bat to face the Reds' Bucky Walters. Bucky lost control of a pitch which struck the Giant shortstop squarely in back of the head. There was a crack that sounded like bat meeting ball, and the ball caromed off Jurges' head and bounced beyond the pitching mound. The crowd of almost 53,000 cringed in horror as Billy collapsed at the plate. Walters was one of the first to reach Jurges, fear in his eyes and a tremor in his voice. "I'm sorry, Billy," he muttered over and over again. Although there was no fracture, Jurges suffered a severe concussion and he would be out indefinitely.

Despite the loss of Jurges, July 4th found the Giants still in third place, only five games behind the league-leading Dodgers. Durocher's club was sparked by the addition of rookie shortstop Pee Wee Reese, the sterling play of Dixie Walker, the "People's Cherce," and a solid pitching staff of Whit Wyatt, Luke Hamlin, lefty Vito Tamulis, Hugh Casey, Tex Carleton, Curt Davis, the not-yet-washed-up Freddy Fitzsimmons, and Tot Pressnell.

The Giants faltered after the All-Star game, won by the National League 4 to 0. The hitting and pitching were spotty, and the defense was severely handicapped by the absence of Jurges. As July ended, the Giants had fallen 12 games behind the Reds and eight behind the Dodgers.

Ott's drastically reduced home run and run production totals had convinced many of the writers and fans that his days of stardom, if not his career, were coming to an end. In their desire to express their fondness for him and their appreciation of his 15-year contribution to the New York baseball scene, a "Mel Ott Night" was planned for August 7. A crowd of almost 54,000 filled the Polo Grounds to honor the Giant captain as the Giants took on the Dodgers. Ott, usually the focal point of horseplay and friendly needling among his teammates, sat alone in a corner of the dugout nervously twisting a piece of twine and dreading the thought of making a speech before such a large crowd.

A gift-laden table was brought out for the ceremonies. Covered with a Giant banner embroidered with Mel's familiar "4," the table was unveiled to reveal a sterling silver set of 208 pieces and a sterling silver tea service. This was the fan's gift, presented to Ott by New York sports commentator Paul Douglas, who attained greater fame years later as a movie and stage actor. Hubbell, on behalf of the Giants, gave Mel a set of matched golf clubs and bag. Then John Drebinger presented Ott with the first life membership card of the New York Baseball Writers Association to be given to a ballplayer. Brushing back tears, Master Melvin thanked his admirers briefly but sincerely, "not only for these gifts but for the loyalty you have shown me in all these years."

The game had an Auld Lang Syne quality as Hubbell started for the Giants and Fitzsimmons and Mancuso formed the Dodger battery. But unfortunately for the Giants, the final score reflected the current reality as Hubbell was knocked out of the box, Ott was held to a single (although he made a great running catch on a Dolph Camilli drive to the bullpen), and Dixie Walker belted out four hits in leading the Dodgers to an 8 to 4 win.

By Labor Day, the Giants had dropped to fifth place, 17½ games behind the Reds. The club's difficulties on the field were matched by its deteriorating relations with the press. Stoneham was popular enough with the writers and Secretary Eddie Brannick had long been one of their favorites. But Terry came across as a cold, unfriendly man, and he reinforced this notion by closing the clubhouse to the press and discouraging the players from talking to writers. Terry's practice was to receive reporters in an annex of his office in the Polo Grounds. Writers had to climb a flight of stairs, descend another flight, pass a special policeman, then remain in a waiting room until Terry got around to coming out.

Interviewing a player was comparable to visiting a relative in jail as Tom Meany described it: "If a writer wanted to talk to any particular Giant player, he had two alternatives. He could wait until the player showered and dressed after a game and pounce upon him like an autograph hound. Or the writer could send in word through the policeman that he wanted to speak to a player. Then he could interview the player through a crack in the door with the same privacy you would find in a prison." This presented a severe problem to the writers, and it was reflected in the increasingly poor press the team received. Of course the club's poorest showing since 1937 stimulated press criticism and demand for a change, but much of it also stemmed from Terry's long-standing difficulties with the writers.

The club fell apart completely in September, finishing the season in sixth place, 27½ games behind Cincinnati. The pennant-winning Reds did not have to contend with the Yanks in the Series; they beat the Detroit Tigers in seven games.

Despite the Giants' dismal flop there were some individual bright spots. Schumacher was fourth in the league in strikeouts. Lohrman tied for the lead in shutouts with five, and Jumbo Brown shared the lead with seven saves. Babe Young's first full season as a regular was a success as he ranked fifth in runs-batted-in. Danning was among the leaders in batting until the last six weeks of the campaign when he tired and his hitting tailed off. And Ott, even with his hitting and eyesight problems (he ceased wearing glasses within a few weeks after trying them), ranked second in walks and led the Giants in home runs with a late season surge.

Over the winter the Giants picked up Gabby Hartnett as a player-coach. Giant writers and fans speculated that the move was a prelude to Gabby's eventual succession of Terry. But Terry played it straight, stating that "Gabby will make a good coach and I think he can catch enough games to give Danning and O'Dea some rest."

When the full Giant squad reported to Miami in March, there were few new faces. Outfielder Morrie Arnovich had been purchased from the Reds. Infielder Joe Orengo and righthander Bob Bowman had been obtained from the Cardinals. Stocky, young righthander Ace Adams was brought up from the minors. Terry had picked up ex-Yankee Bump Hadley and rehired pitching coach Dolph Luque, who had been out of the game since leaving the Giants after the 1937 season. But Giant fans who expected a major overhaul of the team were keenly disappointed.

The tentative regular infield included Young, Whitehead back at second, the headache-plagued Jurges at short, and Orengo at third. The infield reserves were McCarthy, Chiozza, and Witek, who had not satisfied Terry completely. The outfield starters were expected to be Arnovich in left, Rucker in center, and either Ott or Demaree in right depending upon how Ott looked after his sub-par year. Bob Seeds had been sold to Baltimore, but Jo-Jo Moore and Buster Maynard were still on hand. The catching corps included Danning, Hartnett, and Ken O'Dea. Hubbell, Schumacher, Melton, Gumbert, Lohrman, and Bowman were the likely starters. Youngsters Ace Adams, Bob Carpenter, and Johnny Wittig and veterans Hy Vandenberg and Paul Dean were potential starters. For relief pitchers there were Jumbo Brown, Jim Lynn, and Hadley.

Danning signed after a stubborn holdout. Terry surprised everyone by assigning Harry to left field, a position he had never played before. Terry told the unbelieving writers, "Don't worry about our catching. O'Dea can handle it for most of the games and Hartnett should be able to start 40 or 50 games." Actually the writers were more dubious about Danning's ability as an outfielder than O'Dea's or Hartnett's ability to replace him. Their concerns proved justified, as Danning provided ample evidence that the outfield was not for him, and the experiment was abandoned in a few weeks.

There were some bright spots. Rucker seemed more assured and effective than in his rookie year. Babe Young was hitting and fielding well. Ott, without benefit of glasses, was hitting the ball solidly and giving every indication of having regained his old form, and Terry announced that Mel would start the season in right field. Hartnett had slimmed down considerably and was in his best condition in years.

In a poll of National League managers, the Reds were picked to win the pennant again and the Giants were relegated to sixth place. Terry claimed unconvincingly that the team "had improved in every department and would give a good account of itself" as the season began.

The 1941 season was almost a carbon copy of the 1940 campaign. Although the Giants were in third place by Memorial Day, they were 8½ games behind the league-leading Cardinals. The hitting had improved with Ott back in form, but the pitching was poor and the infield erratic with Jurges still suffering from his head injury.

Before the Giants began their first western trip, Terry released Hy Vandenberg, Bump Hadley, and Paul Dean. Then, while the team was in St. Louis, he traded Harry Gumbert to the Cardinals for Bill McGee. A big, apple-cheeked righthander, McGee had been a winning pitcher for the Cards in 1939 and 1940 after bouncing around the Cardinals' farm system for several years, but had been ineffective in 1941. The quiet Gumbert had been the Giants' biggest winner over the past three years and most of the writers and fans were unhappy with the deal.

A few days later Terry bolstered his infield by obtaining Dick Bartell from the Detroit Tigers. Many of the players were amused as Bartell was assigned the locker next to Jurges, one of his long-standing adversaries.

For the first time the effects of the stepped-up war in Europe began to be felt at the ball parks. The draft had begun in late 1940, and several major leaguers, notably Hank Greenberg and pitcher Hugh Mulcahy, either were in the service or would be in uniform before long.

The serious nature of the war was driven home to the fans dramatically during a night game with the Braves on May 27 at the Polo Grounds. That night President Roosevelt delivered one of his famous fireside chats, proclaiming an "unlimited emergency" and the U.S. intention of resisting further Nazi attempts to stop or destroy Allied vessels. With Schumacher facing the Braves' Manuel Salvo, in a 1 to 1 tie, Umpire Jocko Conlan shouted "Time!" For 45 minutes the crowd sat in engrossed silence listening to the President's solemn voice booming out of the loudspeakers atop the center field clubhouse. The players sat on the stairs leading up to the clubhouse or leaned out the clubhouse windows overlooking the field, the game ignored as the national emergency commanded attention.

A few weeks later, a night game with the Pirates in Pittsburgh was stopped temporarily in the fourth inning so that the fans could listen to the fight between Joe Louis and Pittsburgh's Billy Conn. The game had to be called after 11 innings, tied at 1-all, because of a league rule prohibiting starting an inning after 11:50 P.M. Terry was furious, telling reporters that he could see halting a game to hear an important Presidential address, "But hell, not for a prize fight. They might as well hold up the game to listen to a Jack Benny or Bob Hope radio show."

The Giants were in third place on July 4, nine games behind the first-place Dodgers. After the All-Star game, won by the American League on Ted Williams' dramatic last-inning home run, the Giants began to lose ground to the leading Dodgers and Cardinals. Jurges, still suffering the effects of his beaning, returned to the lineup, and Bartell moved back to third base replacing Orengo. Hubbell, now a spot starter, won his seventh straight game. But it was clear that the team could not overtake the leaders, and Terry was the first to admit it. Demaree was sold to the Braves and the Giants bought a big Minneapolis outfielder, Babe Barna. Barna, formerly with the Philadelphia Athletics and leading the American Association in hitting, joined the Giants at the end of the season.

The team collapsed completely on its third western trip, winning only two of 13 games and returning home in fifth place, 16 games off the pace. During the trip Terry told the writers that he would have a "sensational" announcement the following day. The writers speculated all night about the announcement. Several were sure that Hartnett would be named to take over the club. Whatever Terry had in mind fell through though, because he told the writers that he had "reconsidered" and no announcement would be made.

It was learned later that Terry had planned to announce his resignation in Pittsburgh. He had called Stoneham in New York and told him of his intended announcement. The owner flew out to Pittsburgh immediately and talked Memphis Bill into remaining. Stoneham told the writers shortly after that there would have to be a general housecleaning in 1942. He added that only Hubbell, Ott, Young, and Rucker were sure of their jobs and that Terry would remain as manager "as long he wants."

Terry employed an old McGraw era stratagem in an attempt to loosen up his shellshocked troops. Johnny Wittig recently described it:

> We traveled to Boston and lost both ends of a Sunday double-header. After the second game, Bill jumped on a trunk in the clubhouse and hollered, "If I catch anybody out of the hotel after twelve o'clock tonight, it'll cost you $500." Well, everyone got in early that night because we knew he and Pancho Snyder would be up waiting for us in the lobby. We made another swing around the league, wound up in Boston on a Sunday, and got thumped again in a twin bill. After this one, Bill was back up on that trunk yelling, "If I catch anybody back in the hotel *before* two o'clock and *sober*, it'll cost you $1,000!"

Several new Giants received their baptism of fire in the fading weeks of the season. Babe Barna joined the club in September and homered on his first trip to the plate as a Giant. Sid Gordon, a stocky Booklyn native, played his first Giant game a few days later, singled in his first at bat, and was promptly picked off first. Several new pitchers—Dave Koslo, lefty Tom Sunkel, Rube Fischer, Harry Feldman, Hugh East—saw action.

The Giants completed the season in fifth place, a whopping 25½ games behind the Dodgers, who outfought the Cards for the pennant. Individually, Ott, Young, and Rucker were among the offensive league leaders. Ott was second in home runs and third in bases on balls. Young was fourth in homers, second in runs-batted-in, and fifth in total bases. And Rucker, despite a few bad hitting slumps, was third in doubles.

Just before the season ended, Hartnett was released. Terry said, "Gabby was a big help to us and we turned him loose so that he would be free to negotiate for a manager's job. If he doesn't land what he wants, he's welcome to come back with us as a coach." One writer commented wryly, "What a hell of a way to treat a guy after *we* appointed him manager. Where does that leave us?" Giant fans wondered the same thing as they watched the Dodgers lose to the Yanks in a new, less satisfactory, version of a subway series.

10

Changing of the Guard

Stoneham and Treasurer Leo Bondy arrived in Jacksonville, Florida, on December 1 for the annual minor league convention determined to force a showdown with Terry. Jerry Mitchell of the *New York Post* reported that both men were set to ask Terry what he would take "to leave quietly and let them name somebody else as manager for next season, possibly either Dick Bartell or Billy Jurges." As Mitchell saw it, Terry was equally determined to make one final effort to get into the front office, obtain a new contract as manager for three years or more, or stay on to complete the last year of his contract as manager. After considerable discussion in Jacksonville, Stoneham and Terry worked out what appeared to be a happy solution.

Also on December 1, Mel Ott left for the convention from his home in Metairie, a suburb of New Orleans. He enjoyed the company of baseball people and had attended these meetings several times in past years just for a social break in the long off-season. But this time Ott had some things on his mind. He faced a heavy pay cut and the bitter gall of seeing a younger man—Babe Barna—coming along fast after his job as regular right fielder for the Giants. Worried about the size of the cut he'd have to take, Mel went to Jacksonville with a view to putting up an argument. But he was so humble about his odyssey that at first he hesitated about barging in on Stoneham and Terry. Apparently bent on stalling for time, so he could frame some pointed arguments, he was lunching by himself down the street from the hotel when Stoneham and Terry decided that he'd be the new manager. After making their decision, they put in a call for Ott at his home and were completely surprised when Mrs. Ott told them that Mel was in Jacksonville.

"I have a new job for you, at more money," Stoneham told Ott as Mel entered the Giants' suite. Stoneham smiled at Terry and told Ott what the job was. Dumbfounded, Mel looked from Terry to Stoneham and then said, "You aren't kidding, are you?" Thinking of the man he was being asked to replace, he looked at Terry again. "Go on, son, take it," Terry said. "I want you to take it." Ott thought a minute, then said soberly, "I guess a fellow couldn't refuse a chance like this, could he?" He called his wife to tell her the good news, shook hands all around, and sat down weakly in a chair.

Stoneham called Toots Shor at his midtown restaurant in New York. "Hello, kid, I've got swell news for you," said the jubilant Stoneham. "Ottie is my new manager. Yeah, Ott. I need a drink. Wait a minute, here's Mel." "I can't believe it," bubbled Ott. "Isn't it wonderful? That's right, I'm the man."

"Ott the Giants' new manager?" someone asked. "What's going to be done with Terry?" Toots answered, "Jeez, I forgot to ask." He hesitated a moment, then shouted, "Who cares anyway? Ottie's the new manager now."

That afternoon, December 2, the news was released to the press. Ott had been named the new manager, and Terry was now the general manager in charge of farm and scouting operations. Reporters agreed that the sudden change amounted to a victory for Terry and a big break for Ott as well as for the ball club and its fans. Terry finally was rid of the manager's role which had irked him for the last few seasons. He was now in the front office with a two-year contract at $30,000 a year, instead of the one year remaining of his old contract of $42,500. Ott had been rewarded with a job he hoped to have some day but never as soon or as sudden as this. He picked up $7,000 more than his 1941 salary with a two-year contract at $25,000 a year.

The reaction to Ott's appointment was predictably favorable. Larry MacPhail thought the Giants had made two good moves. "They moved Terry up to the front office where he ought to do them a lot of good and they made a smart choice in picking Ott. Both moves are bound to help the club. The only thing is that being a player-manager from the outfield is a difficult job. Ty Cobb and Tris Speaker, the last ones to do so, found that out." Leo Durocher added, "Yeah, I'll bet he winds up as a bench-manager long before the season is over."

The writers were pleased. They were happy to see one of their favorites move up. They also anticipated that covering the Giants would be fun again as it was during the McGraw days and in the earlier years under Terry. Ott cheered them further with the promise: "No longer will writers be discouraged from sitting on the bench. No longer will players be told not to talk to newspapermen. Nor will it be necessary to get a pass from the manager to see a player in the clubhouse after a game. As for myself, you will find me available every day, at all times."

The Giant players were pleased. Several sent Ott congratulatory telegrams or called him to tell him that they were looking forward to playing for him. Many fans, both in and out of New York, were happy for him. A group of Ott's hometown friends wrote an open letter to him in a three-quarter page advertisement in a New Orleans paper. They expressed their appreciation of his qualities as an athlete and sportsman and their gratification at his promotion. Even some Dodger fans expressed their fondness for Ott, many also bemoaning the fact that Terry would no longer be on the field as a ready target for their boos.

Before leaving Jacksonville for New York and then on to Chicago for the major league meetings, Ott dispelled all thoughts that he simply would be Terry's lieutenant on the field. He immediately countermanded three of Terry's decisions. First was the removal of Harry Danning from the trading block. Terry had long admitted that he had not hit it off with the catcher, but Ott said he knew Danning well enough to be confident that under the new regime Danning would have his best year. Second was the acquisition of Hank Leiber from the Cubs for Bob Bowman and cash. Terry had not gotten along with Leiber either and had no interest in getting the big slugger back from Chicago. Third was Ott's dismissal of Pancho Snyder as coach. Terry originally had intended to retain Snyder, but Ott asked Memphis Bill to take Snyder into his own department as a scout or minor league manager. Terry took good care of his long-time coach, elevating Snyder to the manager's slot with the Jersey City Giants.

On December 7, as the Giant party was getting settled in its hotel suite in Chicago, the Japanese bombed Pearl Harbor. All bets were off. Prospective player deals appeared almost forgotten as the baseball officials waited for the government's response. As Ott put it: "We just can't be concerned with who will be drafted. Baseball will be glad and proud to see its men, just like the rest of the youth in the land, called up. Our boys are enlisting, the country is at war, and that's all that matters. We'll carry on our game as best we can, but everything else but the war effort is secondary."

Convinced that they could not conclude a deal for Cookie Lavagetto because of the tightened manpower situation, the Giants bought third baseman Bill Werber from Cincinnati for $20,000. The trim Duke University graduate had batted only .239 in 1941, but he was an accomplished third baseman, something the Giants had lacked for years. Ott regretfully sold his old friend Jo-Jo Moore along with Morrie Arnovich to Indianapolis. A few days later Burgess Whitehead also was sent to the minors as Ott continued to clean house.

The most important deal came in midwinter when the Giants obtained Johnny Mize from the Cardinals for Bill Lohrman, Ken O'Dea, Johnny McCarthy, and a bundle of cash. This trade made a big impression on writers and fans alike because of its underlying meaning as well as for the power Mize brought to the Giants. The Dodgers at the time were hot on the trail of Mize, and MacPhail had seldom failed to land a player he wanted. But Ott had firmly informed Stoneham that he wanted Mize at almost any cost, and Stoneham, perhaps as amazed as anyone at Mel's forcefulness and persistence, parted with an estimated $50,000 (a lot of money in those days) for "The Big Cat," the players' nickname for the big Georgian with the smooth swing.

The uncertainty as to baseball's position was clarified during the winter. Commissioner Landis wrote to President Roosevelt, not seeking any preferential treatment for the game, but to ask what its role should be with the nation at war. FDR wrote the Commissioner that there would be no "work or fight" edict as there had been during World War I. The President stressed the importance of the game as a public morale-builder and urged its continuance so long as the clubs could field teams.

In the remaining few weeks before spring training, Ott was honored at two big dinners. The New York chapter of the Baseball Writers of America presented him with an award for "outstanding service to baseball over a period of years." In accepting the award the new Giant manager first paid tribute to his predecessors, McGraw and Terry. He concluded with, "I know the kind of baseball New Yorkers want and I promise to give it to them."

Ten days later the New Orleans Quarterbacks Club, several hundred strong, gave Ott a testimonial dinner at which they praised their fellow townsman to the skies. Ott responded simply and eloquently: "A few years ago I left for spring training as a rookie with the good wishes of all of you. It looks like I'm still a rookie and it's wonderful to know that I still have your good wishes."

The pitchers and catchers reported to camp in Miami in mid-February, and the remainder of the squad reported a week later. The writers immediately detected a different attitude among the players than in several years. Many of them obviously had worked hard to get into shape before leaving for camp. Bill McGee, in particular, had been overweight during the 1941 season and surprised his teammates with his slimmed-down appearance. All the veterans were in a happy frame of mind reflecting their fondness for their new boss and their renewed enthusiasm for the game. Harold Parrott wrote in *The Sporting News:* "Most encouraging . . . has been the attitude of athletes like Hank Leiber, Harry Danning, and Fiddler Bill McGee. I have never seen Leiber work as hard as he has this spring. The big, blond Arizonan is out at the park early every morning, running himself into a lather. . . . Danning, one on whom Terry's rules and regulations never sat lightly, is a different man now. He is anxious to do a big job for little Mel."

As the training season moved along, the team started to take shape. Mize, after taking it easy early in the spring favoring an old shoulder injury, began to round into his old slugging form. Second base was still up for grabs between Connie Ryan and Mickey Witek. Jurges, now the captain in place of Ott, was set at shortstop. Werber looked sharp at third.

Babe Young's draft status still was indefinite, and he, Joe Orengo, and Bartell were the backup infielders.

In the outfield Ott, despite his responsibilities, was hammering the ball and looked ready for a good season. Leiber replaced Rucker in center as Johnny had a poor spring. Willard Marshall, an unsung, rangy youngster up from the Southern Association, had become the apple of Ott's eye with his hard hitting and willingness to learn. He was picked to start the season in left field. Babe Barna, Sid Gordon, and Rucker were the reserves as Maynard had been optioned to Jersey City. Danning, of course, was set behind the plate, with Ray Berres his backup man.

The pitchers included the two elder statesmen, Hubbell and Schumacher, Melton still seeking to regain his old form, and bespectacled Bob Carpenter who hoped to improve upon his 11-victory season in 1941. The two new lefthanders, Tom Sunkel and Dave Koslo, and righthanders Hugh East, Harry Feldman, and Rube Fischer were other potential starters. Ace Adams, of course, was the unchallenged king of the bullpen.

As the Giants wound up their annual barnstorming tour north with the Indians, now managed by their new boy manager, Lou Boudreau, Ott told the writers: "I think we'll be improved over last year. We'll score quite a few runs once the weather warms up and Mize, Danning, Marshall, Leiber, and the other fellows get loosened up. The real question is our pitching, and only time will answer that one. I really believe we have a colorful club that the fans will like and which has a good shot at the first division, but I've been around too long to predict where we'll finish."

The Giants were picked to finish fifth by the 74 reporters polled by the Associated Press. The Cardinals were picked to win the pennant, with the Dodgers, Reds, and Pirates finishing in that order. Unconcerned about expert opinion, Giant fans and writers eagerly awaited the start of the season to see how their favorites would fare under Mel Ott's direction.

MEL OTT

11

A Good Start

Ott picked Hubbell to pitch the opener against the Dodgers at the Polo Grounds. He was needled by reporters for choosing his old roommate and closest baseball friend to help inaugurate his managerial career. Ott responded, "Sure, you could call it a sentimental choice. But it's downright common sense, too. Hub's the best pitcher on the staff right now. His arm is all right, he feels strong, and I'm convinced he's our best bet." If this told something about Mel's sense of loyalty, it also told something about the weakness of his pitching staff. Great as Hubbell had been, he had not won more than 13 games in any year since 1937.

The Opening Day ceremonies included fiery, little New York Mayor Fiorello H. LaGuardia on the field to present Managers Ott and Dorocher with war bonds, representing 10 percent of their first salary checks. The Dodgers, leading off in the first inning, loaded the bases. Joe Medwick sliced a double to right for two runs, and the Dodgers scored two more runs before the inning was over. Reese gave the Dodgers a 6 to 0 lead with a two-run homer in the fourth inning and that was the end for Hubbell and the Giants for the day. Ott called time, walked in from right field, and took the ball from King Carl without a word.

As Bob Considine of the *Mirror* dramatically described it:

> So Hub turned away from the mound . . . and he started that eternity of steps toward the center field locker room. And the great crowd . . . sensing the rather brave thing Hub had tried and failed at, stood up and cheered the old guy as he trudged along. Eager hands reached down over the barriers as Hub went past the bleacher section and tried to touch him. He shied away, with his head down, and walked up the steps. He was the picture of Defeat, the symbol of a man who had

89

tried to do something for a friend of many years, and had failed. It was too much to ask of an old arm. (But) to us, it was as overwhelming a scene in sports as some of Hub's miraculous deeds of bygone years, when he had it.

The next day Melton beat Higbe on young Willard Marshall's grand slam homer, but Dave Koslo lost to Ed Head in the third game. Ott's club had lost its first series under his leadership and to their hated interborough rivals at that.

There was another managerial first for Ott the next day in Boston. He was ejected from the game, along with Schumacher and Captain Billy Jurges, by Umpire Ziggy Sears in a tough loss to the Braves. Schumacher was fined $50 and suspended for five days for pushing the umpire after Sears' delayed call in ruling a Boston runner safe. Ott was still sizzling the next morning. He complained that he had not said a word to the umpire before Schumacher's ejection and that all of his remarks before that had been intended to calm down Prince Hal. The next day found Stoneham at the Braves' park in a box seat behind the Giant dugout to see for himself whether his players received any more "pushing around."

The Giants bounced back to slug out six wins in their next nine games. The pitching was unsteady, but the Giant rooters enjoyed the team's explosive attack. After years of watching the club struggle for each run, the fans particularly appreciated the Giants' newly created "Dynamite Division," comprising Ott, Mize, Marshall, Leiber, and Danning batting in the third through seventh positions.

With Ott now responsible for running the club, "Ottville" in the right field stands became even more densely populated as closer proximity to the manager apparently gave the fans more of a feeling of being part of the game. As Larry MacPhail had predicted, Ott found the job of managing from the outfield exhausting. The added mental and nervous strain was difficult enough; but to this was added the physical burden of trudging in to the infield several times a game on those stumpy legs. It seemed as though half of each game found Ott either at the mound cajoling, encouraging, advising, or removing a pitcher or elsewhere in the infield registering a complaint on an adverse umpiring call.

Master Mel, still a player at heart, had a tendency to give a pitcher every opportunity to work himself out of trouble. It was a long way in from right field to the mound, frequently long enough to permit his empathy for the pitcher to override his better judgment. He came in one day presumably to take Schumacher out of a game against the Dodgers with men on first and third and the dangerous Camilli at bat. Schumacher figured he was gone as soon as he saw Mel start in from the outfield. But by the time Ott reached the mound he had changed his mind. "You've been pretty lucky getting Camilli out," he told Schumacher. "I'm gonna let you pitch to him." Hal then walked Camilli, filling the bases and

90

bringing Ott in again. (This was long before the rule which requires a pitcher's automatic removal after two trips to the mound in the same inning by a manager or coach.) This time, to prevent another change of mind, Ott wigwagged Harry Feldman in from the bullpen before he went to the mound.

After one of the early season games Ott talked with a writer about the problems of managing and playing at the same time. He admitted, "I'll tell you, I'm really getting an education even after all my years in the game. You know, sometimes the decision as to when to pull a pitcher can be murder. My instinct tells me to take him out, but my desire to give him another chance or build up his confidence tells me to leave him in. Another problem is to anticipate plays and circumstances and make the right move in time. Every manager faces these problems, but they must be more difficult when you also have to concentrate on the game as a player. The other day Pete Reiser hit a fly ball out to me when I was thinking about something else and it actually startled me until my normal reflexes took over."

There was another, more visible, sign of the stress of managing. Ott had always been in the habit of tapping the outfield sod gently with his right foot as he played his position. After a few games the small bare spot in right field began to grow in diameter under the pressure of his nervous foot-tapping. One of the fans teased Ott about ruining the velvety sod. Mel grinned and drawled, "You're kidding me about it, but the groundskeeper is threatening to ask Stoneham to bill me for the resodding cost if I don't cut it out!"

The Giant writers were welcomed to the clubhouse after home games, a complete reversal from the Terry era. Ott, still in uniform, sat and chatted with them, candidly discussing his strategies, players, and problems. He even poured a drink for those who desired it. The writers were free to talk to the players as they showered and dressed. The men covering the team were pleased at the easy accessibility of the boyish Ott and his players, and the favorable press the club received reflected their appreciation.

The Giants closed out their first round of games with the eastern teams by losing a double-header to the Braves at the Polo Grounds before almost 50,000. Still the club had won nine of its first 15 games, and more than a thousand fans jammed Eighth Avenue outside the Giant clubhouse to wish the team well. When Ott came out they let loose a resounding cheer and then dispersed. As Joe King of the *World-Telegram* wrote the next day, "It couldn't be clearer that Mel has resuscitated the old Giant fan who appreciates that Ott is trying hard to give him renewed hope and a run for his money."

The Giants had their problems on their first western trip, losing six games out of 10. Four of the losses were by one-run margins. There were injury problems too. Jurges' dizzy spells returned and Bartell replaced him at short. Leiber pulled a leg muscle and Rucker took his place. After a few games, when it became apparent that Rucker would not fill the bill, he was optioned to Jersey City and Buster Maynard was inserted in center. Ott himself went into a slump. The only bright spots were the powerful hitting of Mize and Marshall and the steady relief pitching of Ace Adams. Desperate for pitching help the Giants reacquired Bill Lohrman from St. Louis, where he had been sent as part of the winter deal for Mize.

The Giants returned home and lost their first game of the season at Ebbets Field as Camilli's late-inning homer beat Melton in another one-run game. The only consolation was that almost $60,000 was raised from the paid attendance for the Navy Relief Society. John Drebinger of the *Times* noted, "It was probably the best-natured gathering in years when the Giants played in Brooklyn. Gone were the jeers that met Terry—only cheers greeted Manager Ott."

The western teams came in for the first time, and the Giants continued to struggle, again winning only four of the 10 games played and slipping down to sixth place. Jurges and Leiber returned to the lineup, but Danning and Werber replaced them on the injured list. Ott continued to experiment, substituting Connie Ryan for Witek and shuffling his pitchers in and out of the starting rotation.

During the home stand New York City civil defense officials prohibited all evening activities which required outside lighting after one hour following sunset. German submarines were operating close enough to the East Coast to be aided by the glow in targeting silhouetted Allied vessels. In effect there would be no more night games for the duration of the war. The New York clubs began to play twilight games—games starting at 7:00 p.m. and continuing through to the curfew if necessary.

As the western clubs left, the Giants' weaknesses were all too apparent. The offensive power was there, but the defense, speed, and above all the pitching were seriously lacking. It was clear that the team did not have the horses to compete seriously for the pennant with the Dodgers and the Cardinals. The team needed some kind of spark if it hoped to finish in the first division.

Ott, the player rather than the manager, supplied a good portion of the spark in a game against the Dodgers as Melton outpitched Ed Head. In the first inning Ott had started the Giants off on the right foot with a two-run homer. But it was his base running that threw some concern and respect into the Dodgers and gave the Giants the lift they needed. In the third inning, with one out and men on second and third, Head walked Ott purposely to fill the bases and set up a double play. Mize slashed a sharp grounder to the sure-handed Camilli and a double play appeared inevitable. Camilli threw to Reese for a force on Ott, but Pee Wee, streaking across the bag in the direction of first base, offered a perfect target. Instead of sliding, Mel came into Reese standing up, a la Pete Rose, sending the Dodger shortstop sprawling. Pee Wee's relay to first base was wild, and two more Giant runs came in.

The Dodgers did not take kindly to Ott's hard-nosed base running. They retaliated by running the bases with special aggressiveness and also resorted to the customary dusting-off tactics which were standard under Durocher. Twice after his rugged base running Ott came to bat, and both times — once with Hugh Casey and then with Larry French — the first pitch was aimed at his head. Ott, hopeful that he had lit a fire under his club, was impassive through it all. In the clubhouse after the game he commented straightfaced, "French and Casey were a little wild out there today, don't you think?"

The Giants wound up their eastern swing in fourth place. With Danning injured and weak-hitting Ray Berres the only able-bodied catcher, the Giants acquired old reliable Gus Mancuso from the Cardinals. Ironically, with this acquisition the Giants had regained the three players involved in the big trade with the Cubs after the 1938 season: Bartell, Leiber, and now Mancuso were all back.

The players were in a cheerful mood as they arrived in Chicago to start their second western tour. Although Ott had no illusions about finishing ahead of the Dodgers or the Cardinals, he was pleased on several counts. The Giants had taken two straight series from the Dodgers. Mize was hitting the ball lustily and leading the league in runs-batted-in. Ott's faith in Willard Marshall had been rewarded, and the rookie was close behind Mize for the RBI lead. Mel had reason to believe that the pitching had stabilized, after much painful experimentation, with Lohrman, Carpenter, Melton, Sunkel, and Schumacher in the starting rotation. All had pitched well except for Schumacher, but Ott felt that the veteran righthander would regain something of his old form. Hubbell was being used as a spot starter. Bill McGee had a bad back and was of little use. Ace Adams as always was a one-man relief staff.

Ott had the personal satisfaction of tying Rogers Hornsby's National League record of 1,582 runs-batted-in during the last game of the home stand against the Phils. The little manager was not hitting for average, but he was getting timely hits and a lot of walks and was on base frequently to be driven in by Mize amd Marshall. And he was still regarded as the best defensive right fielder in the game.

The club did reasonably well on the western trip, splitting 12 decisions and returning home in third place. Mize, Marshall, and Ott continued to carry the offensive load, and Ott broke Hornsby's RBI record against the Cubs on June 4. But the pitching was just fair and the fielding was uncertain as Jurges and Werber appeared to have slowed up considerably and Witek had yet to hit his form. Barna and Leiber were being platooned in center field, but neither man was hitting with any consistency.

93

The western teams came in for the second time, and the Giants broke even despite the loss of Marshall for most of the home stand. Against the eastern teams they continued at the same pace, and at the All-Star game break they were in fourth place, 14 games behind the league-leading Dodgers.

By midseason about 60 major league players were in military uniforms as the country continued to gear up to fight the war. Still there were replacements from the minor leagues readily available. Baseball men agreed that the overall quality of play was not yet unduly affected despite the loss of several top-notch players.

Ott, Mize, Marshall, and Melton represented the Giants on the National League All-Star squad. The game was played at the Polo Grounds with the American Leaguers winning 3 to 1 on home runs by Lou Boudreau and Rudy York. Ott was the only Giant to start and he went hitless. Marshall pinch-hit unsuccessfully.

The Giants opened their third western trip in St. Louis. Koslo was beaten soundly in the first game, and Ace Adams lost a 10-inning heartbreaker on his own wild throw. These losses convinced Ott that the club needed a morale-booster. His solution was to start Hubbell, who had won only one game in the first half of the season. Hub pitched the next day against Howard Pollet, who normally was poison to the Giants. With only a trace of his former stuff but with plenty of savvy, he beat Pollet 8 to 3 and gave the Giants a breather. Although the team lost three of its next four games, King Carl came back and beat the Pirates 3 to 1 with the support of a revamped lineup. Ott benched Werber and replaced him with the peppery Bartell. Even more significant, the slumping Marshall was replaced by Babe Young in a move which reminded the writers and fans of 1937 when Terry brought Ott in from the outfield to replace Lou Chiozza at third base. With the help of Young's potent hitting, the Giants rebounded to take three of their next four games and returned home only half a game behind the third-place Reds.

Back at the Polo Grounds the club held its own against the western teams to remain in fourth place just one game behind the Reds. The home stand began on a surprising note as the Giants bought ex-Dodger Van Lingle Mungo from Minneapolis. The writers, recalling the Mungo-Bartell fisticuffs of the past, chuckled as Mungo was assigned a locker next to Bartell's. One scribe, noting that Bartell's locker was sandwiched in between those of Mungo and Bartell's other old antagonist, Jurges, cracked, "Bartell is like Jimmy Durante—he's surrounded by assassins." Mungo pitched creditably in his first effort but provided little help in alleviating the Giants' pitching shortcomings.

There were more injury problems. Mize missed several games with an injured leg and Young took his place. Jurges' headaches plagued him and Bartell took over shortstop for several games. Leiber's leg still bothered him and Babe Barna was out for 10 days with a pulled thigh muscle. Worst of all, Melton developed bone chips in his elbow which required an operation and sidelined him for the rest of the season.

The biggest disappointment of the home stand came on July 26 when the Reds took a double-header from the Giants. The Giants had moved into third place ahead of the Reds by half a game and there was a near-capacity crowd on hand to see what promised to be an exciting two games. In the bottom of the first inning of the first game Ott came to bat. He was on a home run hitting tear and the crowd buzzed with anticipation. With a one-strike count, Ott took a low, outside pitch which Umpire Jocko Conlon called a strike. The Giant manager stepped out of the batters box and argued the call vigorously with Conlon. Riddle's 0 and 2 pitch was a curve which appeared to shave Ott's chin. Conlon surprised everyone with a booming "Stee-rike—you're out!" Ott immediately turned on Conlon, shouting his disapproval and emphasizing his complaints by pounding his bat on the plate in an unusual display of temper. Suddenly, Conlon turned on Ott and ejected Master Mel from the game with an unmistakable sweeping motion of his arm.

After a few more minutes of impassioned protest, Ott slammed his bat down and began the long walk to the clubhouse, banished for the second game as well as the first under the rules then in effect. As the stocky little manager walked past second base, the fans began to shower home plate with a barage of fruits and vegetables. A tomato intended for Conlon struck Babe Young, the next hitter, squarely in the back. As Ott stomped up the steps to the clubhouse and slammed the door, a shower of beer bottles descended, the fans realizing belatedly that he was out of the second game as well. It was the first game Ott missed all season. After that violent episode the loss of two important games was almost an anticlimax to the disappointed throng.

After the double-header Conlon told reporters, "After what he called me, I had to put him out. I know there were a lot of people who wanted to see him play, but we don't take that from anyone and he can't get away with it just because of the crowd." Ott, still fuming in the clubhouse, said, "It was a terrible call, but it doesn't even matter who was right. Just because I questioned his judgment and punctuated it with a cuss is no reason for throwing me out of a game at the beginning of a big double-header. Durocher throws towels in an umpire's face and little is done about it. I open my mouth once and I'm out."

As the western invasion ended, Frank Graham of the *Sun* wrote about changes in Ott and his team:

> Someone was remarking the other night that a change has come over Mel Ott since he has been manager of the Giants. "Mel used to be such a mild-mannered little fellow," he said, "and now every time I see him he is arguing with the umpires or snapping at the opposing players. And I

never will forget the day he put a savage body block on Pee Wee Reese to break up a double play. What has come over the young man, anyhow?''

The answer to that question comes in two parts. The first is that Ott, feeling that he assumed a heavy responsibility when he took over, is trying in every way he knows to win. The second is that he felt he had to do something drastic to shake up the Giant players. There is no record that he has had to put the blast on any of his own players. But no one, walking into the Giant clubhouse, can have the faintest doubt as to who is boss. He is, as the players show in every move they make and every word they say. Some must ask themselves if this is the same quiet little guy who used to dress over in the corner of the room and seldom had anything to say.

The umpires do not like Mel as well now as they did before. He knows that, but it doesn't bother him in his attempt to give New York the best and most exciting Giant team since McGraw.

The Giants did well against the eastern teams and moved up securely into third place, five games ahead of the Reds. With Mize and Marshall out of the lineup and Danning having a poor year, Young, Ott, Maynard, and Barna carried the offensive load. The defense picked up with Witek's improvement at second and Jurges' return to his old form at short. The aging Hubbell ran off eight straight victories to lead the pitching staff.

In early August it became obvious that twilight games at the Polo Grounds would have to be abandoned as two games with the Dodgers wound up in utter confusion. In the first game Umpire George Magerkurth halted a game in the last half of the ninth inning with the Giants losing by three runs but rallying with two on and none out. Magerkurth called the game at 9:10 p.m. and walked off the suddenly darkened field to the boos of 57,305 onlookers, the largest crowd ever to see a single game at the Polo Grounds. The crowd remained in an uproar until it was quieted by the opening bars of ''The Star-Spangled Banner'' echoing across the field while a solitary spotlight focused on the flag atop the center field clubhouse.

After the game Stoneham said, ''We'll play the twilight game against the Dodgers tomorrow night, but that will be the last one. Playing against the clock this way is too tough.'' As if to prove his point, the next night's game ended in a 1 to 1 tie as Pee Wee Reese's grand slam homer in the top of the tenth was wiped out by the time deadline.

An amusing story accompanied a Giant win over the Phils. The Giants won in the tenth inning when Ott deftly squeezed in Bill Lohrman who was the runner at third. A few days later at Toots Shor's, Comedian Jay C. Flippen, Shor, and several other habitues were sitting around when Ott walked in for dinner. Flippen greeted Ott with: ''Congratulations on that beautiful squeeze play, Mel.'' Ott gave him a sheepish grin and replied, ''Thanks, but it's not something I'm bragging about. Remember when Luque came in from the third base coaching box? It was one out with the bases loaded. Dolph suggested that it would be a good spot for a squeeze play but I told him no, that I would hit away." Ott continued, "So I tap my bat on the plate like I always do and get ready for Johnny Podgajny's first pitch. But just as he delivers the ball, to my complete surprise here comes Lohrman in from third. I made a last-minute stab at the ball and luckily it was a good bunt and he scored. I had forgotten that by tapping the plate I had given the squeeze bunt sign. And yet everybody's been congratulating me ever since on the play."

The Giants retained their firm grip on third place by winning 7 of 10 games on their last western trip. The pitching was solid. Mize was back in the lineup and pounding the ball. Young, back in center field, continued to hit well. Ott moved into the league lead in home runs and belted out his 2,500th career hit against the Cubs. And Witek hit safely in every game of the trip.

There were several items of interest during the last three weeks of the season. Bill Voiselle, a big righthander from Ninety Six, South Carolina, joined the club from Oklahoma City and pitched well in his major league debut against the Phils although he lost the game. The Giants brought up a young catcher from the Appalachian League, Charley Fox, who one day would manage the Giants. Willard Marshall enlisted in the Marines and Babe Young joined the Coast Guard. With the Giants firmly entrenched in third place, Hank Leiber pitched a complete game against the Phillies on September 25—and lost it convincingly. And the next day, the Giants, leading the Braves 5 to 2 in the eighth inning, lost a game by forfeit when overenthusiastic fans overflowed the field.

The overpowering Dodgers and Cardinals fought it out again for the pennant. Leo Durocher's lineup was almost identical to that of the 1941 club which beat out the Cards by 2-1/2 games. This time it was Billy Southworth's team which won by a mere two games. St. Louis was strengthened by the addition of young righthander Johnny Beazley, who won 21 games, great seasons by pitcher Mort Cooper and his batterymate brother, Walker, and the first full campaign of a young player, Stan Musial, whose future greatness was readily apparent. The Cardinals went on to beat the Yankees in the World Series, taking four straight after losing the first game.

The contribution of Ott and Mize to the club's success was reflected in the individual statistics. Despite his burdens as player-manager and 17 major league seasons, Ott missed playing in only two of the club's games, and one of them was attributable to Jocko Conlon's heave-ho. The little manager led the league with 30 home runs and in bases on balls and runs scored, and ranked within the top five in runs-batted-in, slugging percentage, and total bases. Mize was the league leader in RBI's and slugging percentage and in the top five in total bases, runs scored, home runs, and batting average. Ace Adams broke the existing league record by appearing in 61 games. Lohrman ranked fifth in earned runs.

Several writers in New York and around the circuit campaigned unsuccessfully during the last month of the season for Ott's selection as Manager of the Year and Most Valuable Player in the National League. But Giant fans were not particularly concerned when the pennant-winning Southworth received the first award and Mort Cooper the second. They were happy enough with the Giants' resurgence in Ott's first year at the helm.

12

The War Years

The impact of the war effort, relatively light in 1942, changed major league baseball completely during the next three seasons. Through 1942 club owners pursued the usual goals of healthy profits and success on the field. For the remainder of the war, survival was the only real objective.

By the end of the 1942 season, well over 100 major leaguers were in the military services. Almost every day brought reports of players who were either called up for pre-induction physicals or actually inducted. With the decreasing numbers of available players, most of the minor leagues were forced to close down. In early 1942 the Giants owned, or had working arrangements with, nine minor league franchises. By the end of the year only two of the clubs, Jersey City and Fort Smith, remained in operation, and it was considered unlikely that Fort Smith could start the 1943 season.

With this drastic shrinkage in his responsibilities, in December Bill Terry decided to resign. His statement began:

> Some months ago I suggested to both Mr. Stoneham and Mr. Leo Bondy that I did not believe the curtailed activities of the Giants in the minor league field warranted my remaining. I did not feel that I would be able under such conditions to earn my salary. So I suggested that, if it met with the club's approval, my contract for next year be terminated.

To quash any rumors that there was anything more than that to his departure from the Giants after 22 years of continual service, Terry's statement added, ". . . there is nothing but the friendliest relationship between the club and myself. . . ." Stoneham confirmed that Terry was leaving on his own initiative and on friendly terms.

Larry MacPhail, always anxious to be where the action was, had left the Dodgers at the end of the season to enlist in the Army as a lieutenant colonel. He was replaced by the Cardinals' longtime trading master and farm system overseer, Branch Rickey. Significantly, with Terry gone the Giants had no equivalent position in their organization.

In addition to the player shortage, transportation was another serious problem. Airplane travel had not yet come into use in the major leagues except for special occasions, and almost all of the traveling was by train. The government asked top baseball officials to look into ways to reduce transportation needs and suggested that the clubs train near their home cities. It also suggested sharp cutbacks in pre-season exhibition schedules, fewer and longer road trips during the season, and increased use of off-hour trains and day coach facilities. The major league teams took the hint. They found training sites near home, played exhibition games locally, and reduced their travel by a variety of means, primarily by scheduling three eastern-western trips instead of the usual four.

During the 1943, 1944, and 1945 seasons the Giants trained at Lakewood, New Jersey, the little town in which the team had practiced during the Spanish-American War. The Giants and the Jersey City club shared an old, pine tree-covered estate owned formerly by John D. Rockefeller. Their practice fields were laid out on what had been Rockefeller's private golf course, and the players were quartered in the stately, old mansion on the grounds. Bill Corum of the *Journal-American* described it as follows:

> The "Brannick Arms" is so informal and just-one-big-family-like that an occupant of any room in the house can hear, at one and the same time of practically any evening, Maestro Ken Smith practicing on his accordion, Billy Jurges turning the jukebox upside down every few minutes to hear the same tune, Bill Lohrman shaking the pinball machine, and Izzy Kaplan, the demon photographer, rewiring his room so John Drebinger can hear the news on the radio.
>
> If it isn't just like home, it at least makes you wish for home when it's bedtime. Ott doesn't need to check the players in at night. His room is just above the entrance to the hotel, and every time anybody closes the front door his bed jumps off the floor and floats around like a spiritualist's table at a seance.

When the Giants gathered at Lakewood in March 1943 several of the more prominent players were either in the military or scheduled for induction. Young and Marshall were joined in the service by Mize, Danning, Koslo, and Schumacher. Other players expected to hear from their draft boards at any time.

As the club began its first practice drill on a cold, snow-fringed field, it was clear that the team was in for a difficult year unless the other clubs had equally serious manpower problems. The most glaring deficiency was at first base with both Mize and Young gone. Ott tried Babe Barna at the position without success. Then Joe Orengo was moved over from third base. The rest of the starting infield included the improved Witek at

100

second, a slowed-up and headache-ridden Jurges at short, and the stocky, unproven Brooklynite, Sid Gordon, at third. Dick Bartell and Connie Ryan were the reserve infielders. Ott, Rucker, Barna, and Maynard were the only experienced outfielders as Hank Leiber had decided to sit out the season on his farm in Arizona.

Danning's loss was a heavy blow. The other catchers were veterans Ray Berres and Gus Mancuso and Hugh Poland, who had been brought up from the minors. The pitching staff included one shining light, reliever Ace Adams; veterans Hubbell, Mungo, Lohrman, and Melton; and several young pitchers—lefty Tom Sunkel and righthanders Harry Feldman, Rube Fischer, Ken Trinkle, Bill Voiselle, Johnny Wittig, Bill Sayles, and a grim-visaged unknown named Sal Maglie.

With the travel restrictions in effect, exhibition games were played only with Gabby Hartnett's Jersey City club and service teams from nearby military installations. As the Giants prepared to open the season in Brooklyn, the AP poll picked them to finish fifth and favored the Cardinals to repeat.

Lohrman lost the opener to the Dodger's Ed Head before a meager Ebbets Field crowd of just over 18,000. Starting his eighteenth season, Ott went 4 for 4 and drove in both of the Giant runs. But the big story of the game was the baseball itself. The new ball in play was seriously flawed. It had the resiliency of an overripe grapefruit and the unpredictable airborne characteristics of a flying saucer. Ott, brushing off congratulations on his hitting performance, commented, "This new ball is really something. I hit several in batting practice that I thought were really tagged but they all fell far short of the wall. In the outfield I couldn't be sure whether I had come in fast enough to make a catch. And the way the balls twist and dip, they're hard to catch even if you're camped under the ball."

A few days later the manufacturer, A.G. Spalding Company, admitted that the balls had a rubber cement of inferior quality. Instead of providing resiliency, the cement had hardened between the wool layers and deadened the ball. The problem was resolved when it was agreed to use the remaining balls left over from the 1942 season until a new stock of higher quality baseballs was available.

There were early signs that 1943 would be a difficult year for the Giants. With the campaign less than a week old, the club moved to shore up the weak catching staff by obtaining slugging Ernie Lombardi from the Braves. The slow-footed "Schnozz" could still hit the ball as evidenced by his league-leading .330 average in 1942. For Lombardi the Giants gave up catcher Hugh Poland and light-hitting Connie Ryan. Ironically, just after the trade Ryan beat the Giants with a ninth inning home run. Big Lom, in unhappy contrast, ended the game by striking out as a pinch hitter with the tying run on base.

101

The Giants went into a protracted slump, losing 16 of their next 22 games and falling to seventh place. The only bright spots were Sid Gordon's solid hitting and dependable play at third base and a few good pitching turns by Wittig, Feldman, Trinkle, and Adams. The club had a poor home stand against the western teams and dropped deeper into the second division. After trying unsuccessfully to bolster his team with trades, Ott told the writers unhappily, "We badly need to make changes but no one wants to trade or sell players. There's plenty of money around but there's an awful shortage of good players."

As the Giants headed west for the first time Arthur Daley of the *Times* described their plight:

> The Giants, it is sad to report, are not a good team at present. With Johnny Mize, Babe Young, Willard Marshall and Harry Danning gone into service, most of the power has deserted and too heavy a burden is placed on Mel Ott's really promising corps of youthful pitchers. Maybe he can straighten out his forces in the West, but he will have to be a master magician to do the trick because he simply has not the men to juggle.
>
> Last year the Giants came to life when Young was switched to the outfield. However, there is no one like the Babe around this season to set up as a Noble Experiment. The legion of Ott admirers hope fervently that Master Melvin can get untangled even though he's snarled up right now.

But the Giants did not get unsnarled, returning from their trip mired deep in seventh place. During the trip Hubbell broke a string of seven straight Giant losses by pitching his final masterpiece. On June 5, approaching the age of 40, he threw a brilliant one-hitter against the Pirates, winning 5 to 1 with Elbie Fletcher's homer the only Pittsburgh hit. This was Hubbell's 250th career win.

The low esteem in which Giant hitting was held was reflected in an experience Tom Meany had in Pittsburgh. While Meany was in the Pirate clubhouse scrounging for news, he noticed a blackboard in Manager Frankie Frisch's office detailing how the Pirates planned to pitch to each Giant. Frisch came into the clubhouse, saw the writer peering into his office at the blackboard, and bellowed, "Hey, Meany, get the hell out of here. I don't want you going back to those guys and telling them what their weaknesses are. Some of those fellows don't even know themselves what they can't hit." The next day, after hearing Meany's story, Ott deliberately made a visit to the Pirate clubhouse to chat with Frisch and, most importantly, take a look at the blackboard. Frisch invited Mel in and talked about old times at considerable length. Ott told Meany later, "Tom, we had a nice social visit but don't think for a moment that I got a look at that blackboard. Frank had pulled a dark shade down over it and every once in a while he would look over at it, wink at me, and go right on talking about something else."

By July 4, the Giants had sunk well into last place. The pitching staff, particularly Hubbell, Melton, and Mungo, was futile. Lombardi was slow rounding into shape, then was out with injuries. Orengo was hitting under .200. Gordon and Maynard had fallen into deep batting slumps. Rucker was ineffectual. Jurges and Bartell were showing their ages. Ott salvaged a few games with late-inning home runs and even led the majors in homers at midseason. But he was having his poorest year—a combination of physical ills, the weariness of 17 major league seasons, and the frustrations that went with managing an undermanned club in a difficult time with little help from the front office.

Personnel changes did not help. Babe Barna was traded to the Red Sox for lefthander Ken Chase, but Chase proved to be no ball of fire. Napoleon (Nap) Reyes, a flashy Cuban infielder, was brought up from Jersey City. After a short stint at third base he replaced Orengo at first base, but there was no discernible improvement. In mid-July, the Giants picked up Joe Medwick from Brooklyn for the $7500 waiver price. Before obtaining him, the Giants had been struggling along with "3½" outfielders—Ott, Maynard, Rucker, and Gordon, who divided his time between third base and the outfield. Medwick, although only a shadow of the powerhouse he had been in his heyday with the Cardinals, had several good games and did manage to hit a respectable .281 after joining the club.

On July 31, the Giants announced a major trade with the Dodgers. Bill Lohrman, Bill Sayles, and Orengo were dealt for Dolph Camilli and fiery righthander Johnny Allen. Camilli was the key man in the deal because of the Giants' difficulties at first base and in producing runs. Ott, while recognizing that Camilli was well past his peak, was overjoyed at getting him—overjoyed until Camilli unexpectedly announced that he did not intend to play out the season. Dolph told the writers, "I haven't been helping the Dodgers and I doubt that I can help any club. Playing for the Giants might be like taking money under false pretenses." After a two-hour meeting with Camilli, Ott disappointedly reported that Camilli would not change his mind. At least no one could question the rugged Californian's integrity as Camilli's decision cost him almost $8,000 in salary. The net result was that the Giants wound up with Allen and $7,500 (the waiver price) since the deal had been made in good faith by the Dodgers. The Dodgers retained Lohrman, Sayles, and Orengo and a considerably lower payroll which, according to many aggrieved Dodger fans, was why Rickey made the deal in the first place.

The Giants dragged on through August, sinking deeper into the cellar and suffering additional indignities. In one game against Manager Freddy Fitzsimmons' Phillies, the Giants tied an old record for futility by stranding 18 men on base in a mere nine innings. Then an injury to Jurges left them with no substitute fielders; only seven able-bodied players were available to man the infield and outfield. Ott, in no condition to play because of a variety of ailments, was booed lustily after a misplay, a fan reaction he had never before received at the Polo Grounds. He was asked about it after the game. Ott replied, "I can't really blame them. The team

103

is doing poorly and I'm playing lousy ball. But if I don't play right field, who will?" A few days later the little manager came down with an ailment announced as a "stomach bug" which forced him to bed for a week. The story around the Polo Grounds, though, was that Mel's problem was a nervous stomach brought on by his impossible problems.

There were only two other noteworthy items during the remainder of the season. Hubbell closed out his great career with his 253rd win on August 18, a 3 to 2 decision over the Pirates. And a lanky New York City native, John (Buddy) Kerr, made his major league debut at shortstop on September 8 and homered on his first time at bat.

As the season drew to a merciful close, Stoneham announced that Ott had been signed to a three-year, player-manager contract at a small salary increase. Stoneham told the writers that he never had any doubt about rehiring Ott despite the team's dismal year. Ott was asked whether he seriously expected to continue playing in view of his .234 batting average. He replied, "I know that I'm well past my peak, but I have to feel this was just a season when everything went wrong. As far as I'm concerned, it doesn't mean I'm through as a player. After all, I'm not even 35 yet."

The Giants lost 98 games and finished last, 8½ games behind the seventh-place Phillies. Individually, Mickey Witek ranked second in the league in hits and fifth in hitting. Even with his subpar year, Ott finished second in homers with a modest total of 18 and third in walks. The redoubtable Ace Adams was first in games pitched and second in saves.

In November Hubbell announced his retirement. The Giants signed him to a long-term contract as farm system director, the position Terry had vacated. When Hubbell took over, the Giant farm system consisted of the Jersey City club, the Class D Bristol team in the Appalachian League, and a small scouting staff.

Terry had remained inactive during the year, tending his farm near Memphis and keeping an eye out for opportunities in the game. But in January he announced that he had abandoned the game for good to become a partner in a cotton firm. Memphis Bill said dourly, "It's (baseball) too cheap a business and it's getting cheaper all the time." Then, completely underestimating the post-war profits and salaries to be made in the game, Terry continued, "With the low salaries they're paying managers, players, and front office men now, there's nothing in the game for me." The ex-Giant pilot said he was not worried about the game's future, concluding tartly, "No business in the world has ever made more money with poorer management. It can survive anything."

The Giants lost several key players over the winter. Buster Maynard, Van Mungo, and Ken Trinkle were called up by the Army. Bartell enlisted in the Navy. Witek and Gordon joined the Coast Guard. And Ken Chase and Johnny Allen decided to forego baseball, Chase to remain on his farm and Allen to stay on his job in a defense plant.

After a few weeks at Lakewood, Bill Voiselle emerged as the potential anchorman of the pitching staff with his blazing fast ball and sharp curve. Voiselle had pitched in a total of six games for the Giants in 1942 and 1943. Ott decided that Adams would be more valuable to the team as a starter. Ewald Pyle, a 34-year-old, curveballing lefthander picked up from the Senators, showed promise. Cliff Melton, still struggling with his ailing pitching arm, was with the team. Two experienced righthanders, Harry Feldman and Rube Fischer, were tentative starters. Two other righthanders, young Frank Seward and 43-year-old Lou (Crip) Polli, were likely candidates for the bullpen. Seward had made a few appearances for the Giants in 1943. The ancient Polli's major league experience, typical of that of many of the day's marginal performers, consisted of six innings of relief pitching for the St. Louis Browns in 1932. The aging catching trio of Lombardi, Mancuso, and Berres were all back.

Ott was hopeful that he had solved his first base problem when he picked up Phil Weintraub from Toledo. Since leaving the Giants in the deal for Burgess Whitehead eight years earlier, Weintraub had ricocheted around the baseball circuit—the Cardinal chain, the Reds, the Phillies, Minneapolis, and other minor league stops before quitting the game in disgust to go into the jewelry business. When that venture failed, Phil returned to the game with Toledo in 1943. Although Weintraub was barely adequate at first base, Ott appeared unconcerned about him as he watched the Chicagoan pound the ball to all parts of the field.

George Hausmann, a 28-year-old rookie, was set to replace Witek. Youthful Buddy Kerr appeared solid enough at short. Nap Reyes had replaced the departed Gordon at third. Other infielders in camp included 36-year-old Billy Jurges and a 30-year-old second baseman, Hal Luby, up from the Pacific Coast League.

There was no shortage of outfielders even with Maynard gone. Ott, Rucker, and Medwick were the returning regulars. Rotund Charley Mead had been called up from Jersey City. Three other outfield aspirants—Bruce Sloan, Steve Filipowicz, and Danny Gardella—were in camp. Sloan was an ex-minor leaguer and a practicing accountant. The broad-beamed Filipowicz had never played baseball professionally although he was well-known around the New York area as a former football and baseball star at Fordham University. Just discharged from the Marines, his chances were enhanced by his raw power at the plate and his invulnerability from the draft.

Gardella had worked in a shipyard in 1943. He was an amusing, colorful, native New Yorker with a blithe, free-spirited approach to life in general and baseball in particular. His temperament and personality reminded the writers of Zeke Bonura and he became an immediate favorite of the press corps. "Dauntless Dan," as he was dubbed by the reporters, was a powerful little fellow who hit the ball with authority but whose every move in the field was fraught with uncertainty. One of the writers, after watching Gardella shadowbox with a routine fly ball, wrote that the carefree young fellow had made a "sensational catch of a routine fly ball." Another scribe wrote caustically about a long drive that Gardella had pulled down "unassisted."

The training season began on an ominous note when Ott's draft board classified the 35-year-old manager in 1-A. This meant that he could be called up for military service if he passed his physical exam. It was rumored that either Hartnett or Hubbell would replace Mel if he were drafted. However, before Ott was summoned for his physical, the military announced that men over 26 would no longer be inducted and the Giant organization and the fans breathed a collective sigh of relief.

Hubbell's first spring as farm system director was remembered for the large number of teenagers who came to Lakewood for a tryout. The reporters wrote of Hubbell's enthusiasm for his new job as he worked hard with small armies of youngsters, all eager to find a place in the Giants' depleted farm system or, miracle of miracles, a berth with the parent club as 16-year-old Mel Ott had found in 1925.

As the chilly training season ended, Ott told the writers that he expected the team to have a much better year than in 1943. As he put it, "Things can't be as bad as they were last year. At least now we have some spare players to go around. Then, too, I think some of the other clubs have been hit a little harder than we were. But don't hold me to any prediction. If there's anything more uncertain than peacetime baseball, it's wartime baseball." The AP pollsters agreed with Ott's evaluation, picking the Giants to move up to sixth place and again projecting a Cardinal pennant win.

Bill Voiselle won the opener against the Braves 2 to 1 on Hal Luby's two-run double. The Giants opened with an infield of Weintraub, Hausmann, Kerr, and Luby, who had won the third base job from Reyes. Ott, Rucker, and Medwick were the outfielders, with Lombardi catching. Characteristic of the times, the turnover was so great that only Ott and Rucker had played in the Giants' 1943 opener.

The Giants took the next four games against the Braves and Dodgers but then, as the pitching sloughed off, the club fell back in the race. There was one memorable game against the Dodgers, before more than 58,000 at the Polo Grounds, that the Giants won by an incredible 26 to 8 score. Some of the individual exploits were spectacular. Weintraub batted in 11 runs with a homer, triple, and two doubles. Lombardi batted in seven runs. Ott equaled his own records by walking five straight times and scoring six runs. And the Giants received 17 walks, six of them in a row, from Durocher's hapless pitchers.

But, other than their potent attack, the Giants had serious problems. The pitching was weak and Adams was returned to the bullpen. Ott missed several games with an assortment of injuries, and Gardella, "iron glove" and all, was brought back from exile in Jersey City and inserted in the manager's place in right field. The usually patient Ott, for the first time since taking over the team, expressed his annoyance publicly at what he considered lackadaisical play. As the Giants began their first western trip, Medwick was benched for lapses in the field.

The Giants won only five of 12 games with the western clubs and returned home in sixth place, 7½ games out of first place. As the trip ended with a double-header in St. Louis, Ott, trying to instill some life into the club, gave one of his old-time performances. Returning to the lineup prematurely, both because of an injury to Rucker and the team's listless play, the little manager played right field in the first game and contributed a triple and a single in a losing effort. In the second game he shook up the lineup. Buddy Kerr was benched. Jurges, who had been playing third, took over at short. Ott moved in to play third base and Charley Mead went to center field. Ott then proceded to beat the powerful Cardinals almost single-handed with a long home run and two ringing doubles.

With the war going well and the Allied invasion of the Continent expected any day, German submarines no longer posed a threat to shipping off the East Coast. Restrictions on night baseball in New York City were lifted and on May 23 the Giants played their first night game in New York since 1941. Voiselle was well on the way to a 2 to 1 win over the Dodgers at Ebbets Field in the last of the ninth. With two out and two on, ex-Pirate Lloyd Waner lifted an easy fly to right center for what appeared to be the final out. Just as the ball landed in center fielder Johnny Rucker's glove, Charley Mead, inserted in right field for defensive purposes, bumped into Rucker and jarred the ball loose. Running with two men out, both Dodger runners scored and Durocher's club won 3 to 2. Ott rushed out to the mound to console the stunned Voiselle as he walked tearfully toward the Giant dugout. The incident reminded the older fans of the 1936 game that Van Mungo lost in similar fashion when Freddy Lindstrom and Jimmy Jordan collided.

The Giants came back to win seven straight at the Polo Grounds and wound up their home stand in fourth place. The rejuvenated Ott continued his comeback with eight home runs during the 13-game stand, although his fielding at third slipped badly and he returned to the outfield "for my own safety as well as for the good of the club." Gardella clouted four homers and several other key hits during the home stand. The Giants moved into a tie for third place after a strong showing against the eastern teams. Voiselle came through with five straight wins and Adams pitched well. But except for a few reasonably acceptable performances by the others, the pitching was horrendous. Melton aggravated his ailing arm and was sent to Jersey City. Fischer, Seward, and Feldman were completely unreliable. Polli's ancient arm gave up the ghost. The last straw came when Ewald Pyle broke his thumb in an off-the-field scuffle in Boston. The infuriated Ott fined Pyle and suspended him without pay until he was able to pitch, a full month later.

The Giants picked up pitchers from every direction. They acquired 6-foot, 9-inch southpaw Johnny Gee from the Pirates where he had done little. Johnny Allen was coaxed back into uniform. Andy (Swede) Hansen and Bob Barthelmes, two young righthanders, were brought up from Jersey City. Jack Brewer, just out of the Navy, rejoined the club. But the revamped pitching staff showed no improvement. In addition, Gardella slumped badly at bat and Ott, tiring of Danny's amateurish fielding, sent the colorful youngster back to Jersey City. Outfielder Leon (Red) Treadway was brought up from the Little Giants to replace Gardella. Then, as a mediocre home stand ended, Ott sprained his ankle badly and was sidelined for three weeks.

The Giants' chance for a decent season ended in the disastrous western trip which followed. The team lost its first 13 games on the trip, tying its longest losing streak since 1903, before McGraw took over. Ott missed every game, and Weintraub was out for the first week of the trip. With the offense crippled, the pitching remained poor and the defense fell apart. Ott's frustration increased as he sat in the dugout helplessly watching his charges lose game after game.

The normally mild-mannered Giant pilot was particularly disturbed at his team's play in a game at Cincinnati. The Giants were leading 3 to 2 going into the bottom of the seventh. With Redlegs on first and second, Kerr was slow in returning to his shortstop position after a pickoff play at second base, and the next hitter drove a bouncer through the vacated area to send in the tying run. With two runners on later in the inning, the Reds' Frank McCormick blooped a fly ball into short left field. Medwick attempted a sliding, sit-down catch, but Umpire Dusty Boggess ruled that the ball had been trapped. While the runners raced around the bases to score, Medwick foolishly held the ball aloft and raced in to protest to Boggess. Ott felt that no runs would have scored in the inning if the Giants had played routine big league baseball, and he fined each man $100 for "inexcusable mental errors." Kerr took the fine without complaint, but Medwick, who had a weaker case, objected loudly to the disciplinary action. Joe admitted later that he had pulled a boner and deserved the penalty.

Before the season ended, there was a good example of the relaxed approach to the rules that prevailed during the wartime years. Medwick, at bat one day against the Dodgers, was hit on the elbow by a pitched ball. He sank to the ground grimacing in pain, then walked over to the dugout, apparently out of the game. In deference to the Giants' shortage of outfielders, the low standing of both clubs in the race, and the desire to display all remaining resources of authentic major league talent, Ott and

Durocher conferred as to what could be done to get Medwick back in the game after he had received treatment. Finally, Durocher agreed that Medwick could re-enter the game later so long as Leo could select a pinch runner for Medwick. Durocher picked the leadfooted Gus Mancuso only because the even slower Lombardi was already in the game. Big Lom, the next hitter, obliged Leo by thumping resoundingly into a double play.

The Giants finished the season in fifth place, with Bill Voiselle the only shining light in an otherwise lackluster Giant campaign. The big South Carolinian, with his distinguishing No. 96 uniform, earned *The Sporting News* rookie of the year award with a 21 and 16 record. He tied for third in wins and complete games and led the league in strikeouts and innings pitched. Ace Adams led in games pitched and in saves. Medwick was third in hitting with .337, and Weintraub was well up in slugging percentage. And the doughty Ott, despite injuries and the strain of managing, ranked second in homers with 26, third in slugging percentage, and tied for third in walks with Stan Musial.

The power-packed Cardinals, who still had the services of Musial, Mort and Walker Cooper, Marty Marion, Whitey Kurowski, and other lesser stars won the pennant by 14½ games over the second-place Pirates. They went on to defeat the outclassed St. Louis Browns in the World Series.

Ott missed the uneventful winter meetings, choosing instead to participate in a tour of U.S. military bases in Europe. He was accompanied by Frankie Frisch, Bucky Walters, and Washington Senator knuckleballer Dutch Leonard. The visit came during the famous "Battle of the Bulge," when the Germans launched a massive counterattack in a last, futile attempt to turn the rising Allied tide against them, and Ott came back with some hair-raising stories.

There were few changes when the team regrouped at Lakewood in March 1945. Melton decided to join Lefty O'Doul's San Francisco Seals rather than take a big pay cut. Johnny Allen retired. Mancuso was released during the winter. Van Mungo was back from the service, while Hugh Luby joined it. Two new young righthanders, Loren Bain and Bill Emmerich, were in camp. Veteran righthander Ray Harrell was up from the minors where he had pitched since 1941 after spending a number of undistinguished years with several National League teams.

The pitching as usual was the big problem. Voiselle and Adams were the solid members. With the others Ott could only hope for the best but expect the worst. He was especially hopeful that Mungo would deliver the big season that each of his managers had envisioned since he had come up to the Dodgers in 1931. The writers referred to this as "Mungo fever," a condition characterized by sheer euphoria after watching Mungo throw his blazing fireball followed by extreme depression when Mungo's determined elbow-bending and erratic performances became too painful to ignore.

There were other concerns about the team. With Mancuso gone, only Lombardi and Berres remained to do the catching, and both men were well up in years. The infield was reasonably well set with Weintraub, Hausmann, Kerr, and Reyes the regulars. Ott was particularly high on Kerr whom he described as "potentially another Marty Marion." But he was concerned about the outfield. Medwick missed most of spring training with a back ailment. The center field job was up for grabs between the untried Red Treadway and shopworn Johnny Rucker. Ott expected to start the season, but beginning his 20th year with the club, he knew that his playing days were almost over.

The Giants opened in Boston with almost the same lineup that began the 1944 campaign. The only exceptions were Reyes, who started at third and slammed out four hits, and Steve Filipowicz in place of the ailing Medwick in left field. Voiselle won the game, 11 to 6, following a memorial tribute to President Franklin D. Roosevelt, who had died a few days before.

Ott's club went on to win 12 of its first 16 games against the eastern teams. Almost all of the players were off to fine starts. Rucker hit safely in every game. Weintraub, Lombardi, and Reyes were hitting for distance. Ott was hitting well over .400 although he was hampered by nagging injuries. Hausmann and Kerr clicked around second base. Voiselle began the season with four straight wins, and Feldman won three games. Mungo and the other pitchers were having difficulties, but Adams pitched brilliantly in relief and saved a number of games.

Early May of 1945 was a joyous time as the Germans collapsed completely and surrendered. The war in Europe was over and interest in baseball picked up again. The Polo Grounds was a particularly happy place as the Giants performed admirably against the visiting western clubs. To top it off, Ott, who was leading the league in hitting, tied Lou Gehrig's lifetime home run total of 494 on May 9 with a long blast off a Cincinnati southpaw, one Arnold Carter. (At that time the only players with more career home runs were Babe Ruth with 714 and Jimmy Foxx with 527.) Lombardi was leading the majors in homers and RBI's. Voiselle had won eight straight and Harry Feldman was 7 and 0. The club was off to a great start.

For the first time in his managerial career, Ott felt that his club had a real shot at the pennant. In 1942 he had surprised the fans with an appealing team which played well above expectations, vaulting from deep in the second division into third place. The 1943 club, shattered by personnel losses, was a hopeless case. In 1944 the team had improved but was never in contention. But this club seemed to have a good chance to go all the way in a league without a dominant team.

The Giants left on their first western swing leading the league by 3½ games and playing at an .800 clip. They split their first 10 games of the tour and moved into St. Louis, their last port-of-call, in high spirits. Voiselle, pitching in the first game, outpitched Blix Donnelly and Harry Brecheen for eight innings and went into the bottom of the ninth with a 3 to 1 lead, one out, and a runner on base. Then, with a no-ball and two-strike count, Johnny Hopp tripled to run the score to 3 to 2 as Ott tapped the sod angrily out in right field. Hopp held at third as the next hitter bounced out to Kerr. Suddenly, a tremendous rainstorm came up and delayed the game for an hour. When play resumed, a cooled-off Voiselle gave up a single to Ray Sanders to tie the game and a triple to Kurowski to lose it.

After the game Ott surprised the writers with the announcement that Voiselle had been fined $500 for "disobeying pitching instructions." The overwrought Giant skipper told reporters, "I've been telling my pitchers they would be fined for not wasting an 0 and 2 pitch. So, with 0 and 2 on Hopp, Voiselle grooves one, and the next thing you know the game is gone." Voiselle's only reaction was to comment lamely that the pitch had gotten away from him. The general feeling among the surprised players and writers was that the fine was unduly severe. But a good deal of the criticism of Ott also was directed at his failure to replace Voiselle after the long rain delay, particularly since the big righthander had pitched more than eight innings.

The Giants returned home in first place by four games and things still looked bright despite the dismal loss in St. Louis that had shaken the entire club. Ott had broken Honus Wagner's long-standing National League record for total bases when the team was in Chicago. Weintraub and Lombardi also were hitting solidly. Voiselle and Feldman figured to bounce back from their slumps, and Ott still was hopeful that Mungo would regain his pre-season form. Mel had soured on Medwick, and he decided to use the ex-Cardinal as trading bait for a badly needed catcher if a deal could be swung before the June 15 trading deadline.

The law of averages caught up with the Giants, and a string of losses against the eastern clubs dropped the team into fourth place, behind the Cards, Dodgers, and Pirates. Ott tried to snap Voiselle out of the doldrums by rescinding the $500 fine, but it was of no help. Feldman, Mungo, and Fischer pitched ineffectively. Weintraub was out with injuries. Lombardi tired and had to be rested. The Giants finally dealt for another catcher, obtaining Clyde Kluttz from the Braves for Medwick and Ewald Pyle. Danny Gardella took Medwick's place in left field and showed the hitting form he had displayed in 1944 as well as some improvement in the field. The only other bright spot was Manager Ott himself. Mel was hitting over .350 and playing every day despite a variety of ailments. But the team was struggling to stay up with the leaders.

In late June the Giants played an exhibition game at the New London, Connecticut, Naval base. Former Cub outfielder Jimmy Gleeson, an officer at the base, raved to Ott about a stumpy catcher on the base team. Ott was equally impressed by the awkward youngster's fluid swing, his ability to connect solidly with any pitch near the plate, and his obvious baseball savvy. Learning that the youngster was a Yankee farmhand, Ott contacted Larry MacPhail, then the Yankees' president and general manager. But if the Giants had any chance to obtain the young man, they lost it when Ott offered MacPhail $50,000 for him. Although MacPhail knew nothing about the obscure farmhand, the offer was high enough to alert him to the young fellow's potential. MacPhail reasoned shrewdly that if the knowledgeable Ott offered that much, the Yanks ought to keep him. The Bronx Bombers did, and Yogi Berra proved to be one of the game's great success stories. Unfortunately, the Giants didn't share in it.

The Giants could manage no more than a split during their home stand against the western teams and clearly had lost their earlier spark and confidence. It was during this period that the club learned that Harry Danning would not be back. Discharged from the Army, Danning wrote Horace Stoneham a letter which concluded dolefully, "I wish I could tell you that I was on my way to New York, but my legs are in such bad shape that I'll have to forget about ever playing ball again." On the brighter side the Giants purchased 19-year-old Carroll (Whitey) Lockman, an outfielder from Jersey City out of Lowell, North Carolina. In Whitey's first major league at bat on July 5, he duplicated Buddy Kerr's feat by hitting a home run. In addition to his hitting, Lockman impressed with his speed on the bases and his fine fielding.

Although the war was over in Europe, there remained a serious transportation shortage as servicemen were returned to the States for discharge or for transfer to the Far East. Thus, despite the end of hostilities in Europe, traveling by the major league teams was still restricted by the government ruling which banned civilian use of Pullman sleepers on trips under 450 miles. For example, before the Giants left on their second western trip, Secretary Eddie Brannick noticed that the Giants were scheduled to play a Saturday afternoon game in St. Louis starting at 3:00 p.m., followed by a double-header in Chicago the next afternoon. The Giants requested the Cardinals to move the Saturday game up to 2:00 p.m. so that the Giants could make the last evening train at 6:00 p.m. from St. Louis to Chicago. Otherwise, the Giants would have faced the unpleasant prospect of sitting up in day coaches during the night, then playing an afternoon double-header.

The club fared poorly on the western swing and returned home in fifth place. The trip was remembered best for one of Danny Gardella's antics while the Giants were in Cincinnati. Nap Reyes was Gardella's roommate. Nap went up to his hotel room late one morning to pick up Gardella and head for the ball park. As Reyes entered his room he noticed the window was wide open and there was a note on the bed from Gardella.

"Dauntless Dan" had written that he was committing suicide because "life is too much for me." Horrified, Reyes leaped to the open window. As he approached it, he almost jumped out of his skin when Gardella's grinning countenance rose up over the window sill. Gardella had been hanging out the window by his arms, several stories above the street, "just for a laugh." Reyes was still shaking when he arrived at Crosley Field for the game.

The Giants returned home and moved back into the first division following three good series with the eastern clubs. After missing a few weeks of regular play with injuries, Ott returned to the lineup and continued to thump the ball at a .340 clip. In a night game at the Polo Grounds on August 1, the little manager clouted his 500th career home run. It was a typical Ott home run, a sharply pulled smash into the upper field stands. Belted off mountainous righthander Johnny Hutchings of the Braves, the ball bounced back onto the field where it was retrieved by Giant trainer Willie Schaefer. Later that night there was a big party at Toots Shor's restaurant to celebrate Ott's milestone.

In early August, about the time the Japanese surrender was being negotiated, there were indications that the Giant front office finally was taking steps to build the team for the post-war period. Stoneham announced the purchase of the Class B Trenton club. This gave the Giants outright ownership of two minor league teams (Jersey City, of course, was the other) and working agreements with four other clubs. The Giants also announced some personnel moves. Righthander Sal Maglie and southpaw Adrian Zabala were brought up from Jersey City along with Mike Schemer, a young first baseman. Roy Zimmerman, another first baseman, was acquired from the Newark Bears, and Weintraub was optioned to the Bears.

The Giants took 10 of 17 from the western clubs at the Polo Grounds and held on to fourth place. But they were well behind the Cubs, Cards, and Dodgers, and their chances of moving up in the standings worsened when the promising Lockman went into the Army. Nevertheless, the club seemed to have regained some of its spark, and the Polo Grounds crowds, swelled by returning servicemen, had something to cheer about. Maglie won his first start on August 14 against the Reds. Zabala beat the Cards in his first start. Ace Adams pitched well in relief. And the club was hitting.

Despite their improved form, the Giants were unable to close the gap on the third-place Dodgers, who swept a four-game series from Ott's club in their first meeting in more than two months. During that period the Dodgers had picked up the ultimate in wartime ballplayers—the inimitable Babe Herman who rejoined the Dodgers after a 14-year hiatus. Since the 42-year-old Herman left the Dodgers in 1931, he had played for the Cubs, Reds, Pirates, and Tigers before joining Travis Jackson's Jersey City club in 1938. After that, Babe had spent several years in the minors, never

113

dreaming that he would be back in the major leagues. Yet here he was, back in Brooklyn, hitting an occasional long ball, taking pratfalls on the field with his old aplomb, and pleasing the Ebbets Field crowds as he had in the old days when Dodger baseball was almost indistinguishable from a Mack Sennett comedy.

For the first time in their history, the Giants went over the million mark in attendance while taking a doubleheader from Manager Ben Chapman's Phillies on September 3. The Giant's best previous home attendance was in 1937, their last pennant-winning year when they drew almost 939,000. But artistically, the club was less successful, finishing the season in fifth place, 2½ games behind the fourth place Pirates.

As late as Labor Day, Ott was hitting well over .320, high enough to rank within the top five hitters in the league. However, during the last western trip persistent lameness in his knee worsened, and he announced that he would not play regularly for the rest of the season. As the season ended, League President Ford Frick presented Ott with a lifetime pass in honor of his 20th year in the league, and more importantly, the Giants canceled the one year remaining on his contract and signed him to a five-year contract at a substantial salary boost.

In that last wartime season a few of the Giants did well individually. Adams finished second in games pitched and tied for most saves. Rucker was fifth in triples. Voiselle was third in strikeouts. And Ott, whose batting average dropped to .308, was fifth in homers and fourth in slugging percentage.

The Cubs, almost the identical team which had finished in fourth place and under .500 in 1944, beat out the Cardinals for the pennant by 3½ games. But they lost a seven-game World Series to the Detroit Tigers, who were sparked by Hank Greenberg, just returned from the Air Corps, and southpaw Hal Newhouser and the colorful righthander, Dizzy Trout. Before the first game of the Series, Chicago writer Warren Brown succinctly put wartime baseball in proper perspective. As Brown sat in the press box one of his colleagues asked him whom he picked to win. Brown looked down at the odd assortment of players warming up, thought how much the caliber of play had slipped during the war, then turned to his questioner and answered sardonically, "I don't think either team can win!"

13

Nice Guys Finish Last

At the winter meetings the Giants acquired Clint (Hondo) Hartung from the Minneapolis Millers for future delivery. The purported feats of the "Pheenom," as he was referred to, were unreal. While in the service, the 6-foot, 5-inch Texan had won all 25 games he pitched and batted a cool .567 in 60 games. Baseball men agreed that he couldn't miss; it was merely a matter of settling him in the right position and giving him a year or so of minor league experience. After hearing a continuing string of stories of the feats of this latter-day Paul Bunyan, Tom Meany commented caustically, "Hartung's a sucker if he reports to the Giants. All he has to do is sit at home for 10 years, wait until he's eligible, and he's a cinch to make the Hall of Fame."

In January the Giants bought Walker Cooper from the Cardinals for $175,000, by far the largest sum the club had ever paid for a player. Big Coop was widely considered the best catcher in the game before joining the Navy after the 1944 season. Ott was jubilant as he told the writers of his high expectations for the big Missourian.

A few days later the club announced the signing of Carl Hubbell to a new five-year contract. When Hub took over as farm system director in 1944, the Giants' had only a few clubs and scouts. Now, with the war over, the club owned franchises in Jersey City, Trenton, and Fort Smith and, within a short time, would purchase the Triple A Minneapolis Millers. The Giants also had working agreements with eight minor league teams and had a dozen scouts beating the bushes for talent.

An unusually large squad reported at Miami, so large that Ott and his coaches, Red Kress, Bubber Jonnard, and Dick Bartell, had their hands full instructing and evaluating the players. There were 25 pitchers in camp alone. In addition to the holdovers from 1945, former pitching regulars returning from the services included Hal Schumacher, Bob Carpenter,

Dave Koslo, and Ken Trinkle. The most prominent of the new pitchers were curveballer Bob Joyce, who had excelled in the Pacific Coast League in 1945; southpaw Monty Kennedy, a wild but promising youngster from Virginia; and righthanders Mike Budnick and Marvin Grissom.

The infield was strengthened with the return of Mize and Witek and the addition of two promising rookies, Buddy Blattner and Bill Rigney. Blattner already had attained some athletic recognition—as a ping pong champion. Rigney, a bespectacled Californian, was a slight, peppery young fellow who one day would manage the Giants. Outfielders Buster Maynard, Babe Young, Sid Gordon, and Morrie Arnovich were back, and Willard Marshall was expected back from the Marines before the start of the season. Cooper would be the regular catcher with Lombardi and Clyde Kluttz the reserve catchers.

In the last several months major leaguers had been approached to jump to the Mexican League, a newly formed, "outlaw" league operated by Mexican customs broker Jorge Pasquel and his brother Bernardo. A few days after camp opened, Danny Gardella announced that he had signed a five-year contract to play in Mexico. Gardella also told the writers that other major leaguers had signed with Pasquel, including Nap Reyes, pitcher Adrian Zabala, and Dodger outfielder Luis Olmo. "Dauntless Dan" said he had been paid $4,500 in 1945 and the Giants had offered him only a $500 raise despite his 18 home runs in 1945. He stated that he had no intention of letting the Giants "enrich themselves" by selling him to a minor league club and that he had decided therefore to take his "gifted talents" to Mexico.

Ott showed little concern over the loss of Gardella, Reyes, and Zabala. However, a month later Sal Maglie, George Hausmann, and reserve first baseman Roy Zimmerman jumped to the Mexican League. Maglie revealed that each player would be paid at least double his 1946 salary plus a $5,000 bonus and $1,000 for expenses. Ott became furious at Maglie when it was learned that the jumping players had placed a call to Pasquel from Maglie's hotel room. Sal claimed that the players had used his phone to call Pasquel collect only because they happened to be in his room at the time. Years later Maglie recalled:

> I was optimistic about making the team that year. I had a good winter pitching in Cuba, and when I came to camp Ott seemed glad to see me. I pitched well in an early exhibition game, but after that Ott didn't seem to know I was alive. Most of the other guys weren't getting the look they deserved either.
> Mel wouldn't listen to me when I tried to explain about the phone call. He accused me of setting up the whole deal, acting as Pasquel's agent. Later he came out into the clubhouse and asked all the fellows if they had been contacted by the Mexicans and if so, what their plans were.

Although several players admitted they had been approached, all assured Ott they would stay with the Giants. Their decisions may have been influenced by Commissioner Happy Chandler's edict that all jumpers would be suspended from playing in the major leagues for five years.

Ott's inability to give each man sufficient opportunity to pitch in the exhibition games concerned him greatly and caused a good deal of grumbling in the ranks as Maglie had reported. In fact, brooding after pitching in only two exhibition games, Mungo showed up at the park one day in what Ott delicately called "no condition to appear on the field." As a result he was suspended indefinitely; there would be no "Mungo fever" in 1946.

As the Giants barnstormed north with the Indians, it was apparent that pitching was still the team's fundamental problem. The catching figured to be first rate after Cooper rounded into shape. The big catcher was happy with his $25,000 contract, double the salary the Cardinals paid him in 1944. Cooper also succeeded Billy Jurges as team captain, as the veteran shortstop had been released and picked up by the Cubs. Ott had settled on a starting infield of Mize, Witek, Rigney at short, and Buddy Kerr at third. The outfield corps of Marshall, Young, Rucker, Gordon, and Ott was slow on the bases and in the field, but it had hitting potential.

Ott, preparing to start his 21st season, hit well in the pre-season games. He frightened everyone on the trip north when he was hit in the head by Mike Budnick in batting practice, but came back to lead the club in hitting as it completed the tour with the Indians and moved into New York to start the campaign. The AP pollsters picked the Giants to finish fifth behind the Cards, Cubs, Dodgers, and Pirates.

The Giants opened against the Phils at the Polo Grounds before an enthusiastic crowd of 40,000, including a large contingent of servicemen and recently discharged veterans. Voiselle outpitched southpaw Oscar Judd to win an easy decision despite the absence of Mize and Cooper. Ott thrilled the crowd in the first inning with a two-run homer that sent the Giants off winging. Never mind that it was one of his least impressive home runs, a looping fly that barely reached the right field seats. Of greater significance, it was number 511 of his career and the last major league homer he would ever hit. The next day Ott dove futilely for a fly ball, injured his knee, and played only sporadically and ineffectively for the rest of the year.

Playing poorly, the Giants suffered a serious loss on April 26 when Ace Adams and Harry Feldman unexpectedly jumped to the Mexican League. Ott told the writers, "They showed up in the clubhouse before most of the other players had come to the park, packed up their belongings, and left immediately. I understand that they flashed a roll of bills totalling about $15,000. Well," he went on defiantly, "I'm missing nothing." Despite his brave words, Ott knew he was missing plenty. Feldman had been erratic but appeared on the verge of becoming a solid winner. The loss of the rubber-armed Adams was a body blow to a pitching staff that needed help badly, particularly relief pitching.

117

As the Giants headed west for the first time, Arthur Daley of the *Times* wrote incisively about the club's organizational problems:

> The Giants are one of the few remaining clubs in the majors which still operate under the archaic system whereby all the duties of running the organization devolve upon the manager. . . . It is a job that calls for a general manager, or a general supervisor who directs the affairs of the entire organization. . . . To hold Ott accountable for the woeful start the Giants have made . . . is uncalled for and unfair. . . . Given the opportunity to concentrate exclusively on directing his Giants, such as (Yankee manager) Joe McCarthy receives . . . and Leo Durocher receives . . . , Mel doubtless would more than hold his own. But the Giants still play it as they did in the horse-and-buggy age, and while there may be something fine, noble and ripe in the Victorian touch, it seems to be getting a little too ripe for even the old-timers.

By Memorial Day the Giants were mired in seventh place. Mize was clubbing the ball and Cooper was back after suffering a broken finger. The infield play improved as Ott finally settled on Blattner at second, Kerr at short, and Rigney at third. But the club was painfully slow afoot, and the outfield was unproductive even after the acquisition of Goody Rosen from the Dodgers.

Most important, other than a few acceptable outings by Koslo, Kennedy, Trinkle, and Bob Carpenter, the pitching was pathetic. Ace Adams was sorely missed. In desperation Ott picked up lefthander Tex Kraus from the Phils, Gene Thompson who had been released by the Reds, and a righthander, one John Carden, who had no professional experience. Kraus and Thompson were of some help, but Carden was cut adrift after a few weeks.

The club stumbled through June making little headway, in and out of last place. Ott's frustration surfaced on June 9 in a double-header loss in Pittsburgh. In the first game Umpire Tom Dunn ejected Ott for complaining about a call on the bases. During the second game, Umpire George Magerkurth bounced him for protesting too vigorously on a tipped bat call against Lombardi. Giant fans, hearing the game on radio or reading about it the next day, could hardly believe it. Their mild-mannered idol, Mel Ott, had set a major league record—the first manager to be thrown out of two games on the same day!

Later in the season Ott and Durocher collaborated unwittingly in adding to the American idiom. The last-place Giants took on the league-leading Dodgers at the Polo Grounds. Koslo won the first game behind booming homers by Mize and Lombardi. In the second game Vic Lombardi beat the Giants despite three more well-tagged homers by Marshall, Blattner, and Ernie Lombardi. The next day Dodger broadcaster Red Barber sat on the Dodger bench before the game kidding Durocher. "Leo," Barber said, "your guys were lucky to split yesterday the way the Giants were hitting, especially those home runs." Durocher scoffed, "Hell, they were nothing, just cheap Polo Grounds specials." Barber continued to needle, "Come on, Leo, be a nice guy and give credit where it's due." Durocher, more adept at giving the needle than taking it, shouted at Barber, "Nice guys! Do you know a nicer guy than Mel Ott? Or any of the other Giants? And where are they? The nice guys over there are in last place!" That was the way Frank Graham of the *Sun* reported the dialogue in his column, and that was the origin of the familiar tough-guy phrase—"Nice guys finish last."

The Giants' misfortunes and inept play continued for the rest of the season. Cooper suffered another broken finger and missed several weeks. Ott continued to try anything to help his pitching staff. He went so far as to sign coach Red Kress to a player contract solely because of the live arm Kress displayed in pitching batting practice. Red's only pitching effort in the majors had been in 1935 when he pitched five innings for the Washington Senators. It took Kress only one three-inning stint to convince Ott that he could not help the club. Mize's hitting was one of the few bright spots. But, here again, the Giants were snake-bit as the big fellow was beaned by the Cards' Harry Brecheen, then fractured his hand in a meaningless exhibition game with the Yanks, then broke a toe in his first game back in the lineup, finishing him for the season.

Years later Mize told an amusing story about the Giants' retaliation against Brecheen after he beaned Mize. The Big Cat's story as reported in Donald Honig's classic *Baseball When the Grass Was Green*:

> Well, after I was hit, Mel Ott . . . told (Monty) Kennedy (who was pitching) "When Brecheen comes to bat, throw at him. Not at his head; hit him in the knee." He's telling this to a fellow who generally had a hard time just keeping his pitches in the ball park. But, son of a gun, when Brecheen came up, first pitch Kennedy hit him right in the knee. Brecheen was out for ten days. That's probably one of the mysteries of baseball, that Kennedy, wild as he was, could hit a guy on the knee with his first pitch.

Even with the Giants out of contention, they attempted to play their traditional role in the Giant-Dodger rivalry as they took on the Dodgers at the Polo Grounds in a three-game series just before Labor Day. The Dodgers and Cardinals were involved in a replay of their ferocious pennant fights of 1941 and 1942, and the Giants had a golden opportunity to pay the Dodgers back in kind for the 1934 debacle.

Kennedy outpitched Kirbe Higbe in the first game at the Polo Grounds. Goody Rosen and Eddie Stanky enlivened the game with a spirited fist fight after Rosen slid into second base with spikes high. Stanky took the throw, tagged Rosen squarely in the face, and the two little gamecocks went at it in fine style as the dugouts emptied rapidly. After several vicious, if ineffectual, blows were exchanged, both combatants were ejected. In the earlier McGraw-Terry-MacPhail days, this would have

119

called for a special squad of police at the park for the next day's double-header. But these were different times, and Stanky and the Dodgers got their revenge peaceably enough by easily beating Voiselle and Trinkle before 53,000. Durocher's club wound up the day only 1½ games behind the Cards, and the Giants had lost an opportunity to salvage something from their dismal season.

A few weeks later Rosen buried the hatchet publicly. On Eddie Stanky Day at Ebbets Field, Goody presented the scrappy little Dodger with a set of boxing gloves. He made the presentation with the lighthearted comment over the public address system, "Take these home and practice with them during the offseason." Then, to the applause of 30,000 fans, Goody added, "Seriously, Eddie's a great player and a good friend of mine—except when he's covering second and I'm coming in." With that, Rosen and Stanky shook hands and refrained from snarling at each other until the game began.

After Labor Day the Giants sank into last place, and Giant fans turned their attention to individual players and performances. On September 9, Bobby Thomson made his debut as a Giant, playing third base and slapping out two hits. Righthander Sheldon Jones made his first Giant appearance and pitched five strong innings after a rocky start. But the current Giant hero was Buddy Kerr. The native New Yorker had developed into a superb shortstop and wound up the season with 52 straight errorless games and 274 chances without an error, breaking records set by Durocher and Eddie Miller.

The only 1946 achievement of note was the home attendance. The last-place club drew 1,234,773 fans, exceeding by far the club attendance record set in 1945. Despite his injuries, Mize finished second in the league in home runs with 22, only one behind Ralph Kiner. Dave Koslo, the staff "ace" with a record of 14 wins and 19 losses, tied for second in the league in innings pitched, third in complete games, and fourth in strikeouts. Ken Trinkle, mopping up where Ace Adams had left off, led the league in games pitched.

As the season ended, the Giants began to clean house. Most important, though, to Giant fans—what about Ott's future? Still tremendously popular, Mel had not managed the Giants to a first division finish since his first year as manager in 1942. The war years were abnormal and could be written off. But what about the past season when the team had finished dead last? It was understood that Stoneham was asking himself the same question. A story made the rounds that the Giant owner had contacted Lefty O'Doul in San Francisco to inquire whether O'Doul was interested in replacing Ott. But O'Doul would not leave his home town.

So, the rumors had it, Stoneham had thought, pondered, and thought some more. He convinced himself that the Giants had an offensive powerhouse coming along, the likes of which the Polo Grounds had not seen in years. The crushing injuries to Mize and Cooper were unlikely to strike the team again, and a disaster like the unexpected loss of Ace Adams was even more unlikely. The club had the potential for defensive improvement, too. And the pitching would improve somehow. Hubbell's farm system seemed about ready to start bearing its share of the burden. Moreover, the National Exhibition Company (the Giants' corporate name) had done well financially, and there was no pressure from the stockhoiders to replace Ott. As a matter of fact, there were four more years to go on Ott's contract, and the additional expense of paying two managers would antagonize the stockholders. And, in the final analysis, how could he fire his friend Ottie, the apple of his eye as a player and one of the finest men—yes, "nicest" guys—Stoneham had ever known? No, the personal and financial pressures favored the retention of Ott, and he would be back to manage the Giants in 1947.

14

The Windowbreakers

Giant fans, anticipating a major trade for established pitching talent, were disappointed when the team assembled at its new spring training base in Phoenix, Arizona. Larry Jansen, a lean righthander who had been a big winner in the Pacific Coast League, and Bill Ayers, a 21-game winner at Atlanta, were in camp. There were also several other undistinguished new pitchers. But, with the exception of Hal Schumacher, who had called it a career, it appeared that the Giants were saddled with the same staff that had labored so ineffectually through the 1946 season.

Stocky Dave Koslo was a solid southpaw starter although not the overpowering type normally considered the bellwether of a serious contender's pitching staff. Bill Voiselle had never been the same since his differences with Ott in 1945. Monty Kennedy had pitched brilliantly at times but he still was wild and inexperienced. Bob Carpenter's arm had been ailing for some time. Mike Budnick lacked control and had won only two games in 1946. Ken Trinkle was a durable reliever, but he was hardly a satisfactory replacement for Ace Adams. Junior Thompson had become a marginal performer. Sheldon Jones owned a live fast ball, but he also had control problems. Lefty Woody Abernathy had done little in his few appearances. Ott was so concerned that he hired old-time pitcher Walter (Dutch) Ruether to work with the pitchers during the training season.

The infield picture was brighter. Mize was a powerhouse at first base. Blattner, Witek, and Rigney were experienced second basemen although none of the three were particularly adept at making the double play. Kerr was one of the best fielding shortstops in the league. The third base job was a three-way battle between versatile Sid Gordon, young Bobby Thomson, and Jack (Lucky) Lohrke. Brought up from Spokane, Lohrke had gained his nickname by his good fortune in narrowly escaping a series of airplane, railroad, and bus accidents.

The outfield figured to improve with the addition of speedy, talented Whitey Lockman. Willard Marshall was rated a solid hitter and fielder although he had been a disappointment in his first year back from the service. Johnny Rucker was still around. Lloyd Gearhart and Al White were young outfielders up from the minors without any major league experience. Babe Young was still floundering as an outfielder because he could not dislodge Mize at first base. Joe Lafata, a promising first baseman-outfielder, was given a chance to make the team. Ott was still on the active roster although there was little expectation that he would play. And then there was the fabled Clint Hartung, who had spent the 1946 season at Minneapolis chasing fly balls with modest success.

The catching appeared to be solid enough. Cooper was expected to regain his old form if he could avoid injuries. Ancient Ernie Lombardi was on hand, and Mickey Grasso was back after a short stint with the Giants at the end of the 1946 season.

After a few weeks in Phoenix Ott told the writers, "This is the first Giant team I've seen in a long time that reminds me of Mr. McGraw's clubs. We have more speed than we've shown in a long time with fellows like Thomson, Lockman, Rigney, and Lafata. We have established power hitters like Mize, Cooper, and Marshall and some of the other boys also can powder the ball. I also like the spirit and morale; reminds me of the old bunch—Terry, Ross Youngs, Lindstrom, Jackson, and the rest. If only a few of the younger players come through we should do all right." As the writers left the clubhouse one muttered to another, "Mel may have something there but you notice he didn't mention there was anyone around who reminds him of Hub, Schumacher, or Fitzsimmons!"

The Giants' exhibition game schedule included a series with Lefty O'Doul's San Francisco Seals in Hawaii before the club began its long barnstorming trip east with the Indians who also had moved their training camp to Arizona. The exhibition games were marked by an unusually severe number of injuries to Giant players. Witek broke his arm and was sent home to recuperate. Jansen suffered a broken cheek bone and narrowly escaped a fractured skill when he was hit by a line drive. But the cruelest blow of all came on April 8 in Sheffield, Alabama. Whitey Lockman, who was playing brilliantly, broke his right leg sliding into second base trying to break up a double play. His season was virtually over before it had begun.

Just a week before the season opened, Commissioner Happy Chandler stunned the baseball world by suspending Leo Durocher for the entire season for "accumulated unpleasant incidents." Giant fans reacted to the hated Durocher's ouster with surprising compassion. In addition to the consensus that the one-year suspension was unduly severe, Giant rooters realized they would miss Durocher in the same way that Dodger fans missed Terry when he left the Giant dugout for good. They had lost a choice target for their boos.

Branch Rickey sought out several baseball men before finding a successor to Durocher. He was reported to have contacted ex-Yankee manager Joe McCarthy and been turned down. There were stories that Bill McKechnie, then a coach with Lou Boudreau's Indians, had been approached. Finally, the name of a prominent Giant alumnus surfaced as a candidate—none other than Bill Terry. But before the fans could react to this potentially astonishing development, Rickey replaced Durocher with a long-time associate, 62-year-old Burt Shotton.

Picked to finish sixth, the Giants opened in Philadelphia with an infield of Mize, Thomson at second, Gordon at third, and Rigney at shortstop in place of the ailing Kerr. Willard Marshall started in right field with Al White in center and Hartung in left. Cooper and Voiselle rounded out the opening game lineup. Voiselle pitched well but lost on a wild throw by Gordon, one of five Giant errors. Hartung belted a double and single, but the big fellow ignominiously bobbled the first ball hit to him. The Giants lost again the next day as Ayers and Jansen in relief were driven from the box in their major league debuts and the Giants committed three more errors.

The Polo Grounders came home to open against the Dodgers and to play for the first time against the Dodgers' widely heralded black rookie, Jackie Robinson. Just before the game Rickey announced the appointment of Shotton. Burt sat in the dugout, Connie Mack-style, in street clothes with a pearl gray hat and a topcoat. Koslo won, despite three more errors, behind a six-homer Giant barrage. John Drebinger wrote of the Giants: "Just where the Giants will finish this season is still a matter over which the experts are at considerable variance. But all are agreed the 1947 cast should prove one of the most colorful in years. They have committed 11 errors so far . . . but Ott seems to have assembled a group of dashing youngsters who are not bothered by misplays. They can belt the ball a mile and run like blue streaks."

The club fell into a slump, and Ott shook up the lineup drastically. He moved Thomson from second base to center field to replace the ineffectual alternates, Gearhart and White. Buddy Blattner took over at second base. Rigney moved from short to third to replace Lohrke, who was not hitting. Kerr returned to shortstop. In left field Sid Gordon supplanted Hartung, who was having his problems at the plate as well as in the field.

Convinced that Hartung was not yet a big league outfielder, Ott brought the "Pheenom" in to pitch in a game against the Braves with the Giants losing 6 to 0 after three innings. Hartung, fast and wild enough to keep the Braves from taking toeholds at the plate, for once really was phenomenal. He pitched six scoreless innings and gave up only two hits. The next day Jansen, in his first start, won a slick six-hitter over the Braves.

The club reacted magically to the changes, winning 14 of its next 19 games and vaulting into first place by Memorial Day. Mize, in particular, was overpowering—clubbing home runs, batting in runs in clusters, and setting a National League record by scoring at least one run in 16 consecutive games. Hartung won his first start, against the Cubs, and then came through with another complete game win over the Reds. Koslo, Kennedy, and Jansen also chipped in with well-pitched games. The fielding improved with Thomson and Gordon playing well in the outfield and with Kerr in top form. Buddy handled 383 chances in a row flawlessly (still the major league shortstop record through the 1978 season) before fumbling a hard ground ball drilled directly at him by the Braves' Bob Elliott.

The Giants' pitching slipped badly in June. Yet, their murderous hitting pulled out game after game, and as the month ended, the club was only 1½ games behind Manager Billy Southworth's league-leading Braves. Then the club fell back as the pitching fell to the depths Giant fans had feared before the season began. Jansen continued to win, but Koslo and Kennedy turned erratic. Hartung, after winning his first four starts with complete game efforts, suddenly lost his touch and couldn't buy a win. To make matters worse, Kennedy was put out of action by a hairline skull fracture.

Ott continued his efforts to deal with his pitching problems. Babe Young was traded to the Reds for veteran righthander Joe Beggs. Bill Voiselle went to the Braves for Mort Cooper. One of the game's foremost pitchers at one time, Cooper had lost much of his effectiveness since an arm operation in 1945. Still, Ott was willing to gamble that Cooper's arm would come around in time. Besides, Mel was glad to unload Voiselle, who had been of little use all season. Voiselle was equally glad to leave the Giants, confirming that he had "strained relations" with Ott for some time. Although some of the fans and writers felt that Ott had mishandled the sensitive Voiselle, it is worth noting in retrospect that the big right-hander did not pitch .500 ball in any season for the remainder of his major league career under other managers.

One other pitcher joined the club during the month. On June 22, the Giants picked up southpaw Clarence (Hooks) Iott from the St. Louis Browns. Winless in six big league games, Iott (immediately dubbed "One Ott" by the players in deference to the manager) joined the Giants in Chicago two days later. Ott greeted him with a hearty handshake and the brisk announcement, "You're pitching today." Two hours later Iott took the mound against the Cubs and with little apparent effort pitched a two-hit shutout to everybody's amazement. Unhappily, visions of another badly needed starting pitcher arriving out of nowhere faded very soon. A few days later Iott lost to the Dodgers, and the big lefty won only two more games during the rest of the season.

By the All-Star game break the Giants were in third place, but only because the powerful attack continued to bail out the weak pitching staff. Ott's club broke a National League record by homering in 16 straight games with a total of 37 home runs during the stretch. After the first 77

126

games (half the season), the Giants had hit the remarkable total of 118 home runs, and on August 2 they broke the old Giant record of 144 set in 1930. The league club home run record for a season at that time was 171, held by the 1930 Cubs of the Hack Wilson-Gabby Hartnett era. The American League record of 182 was held by the fearsome Yankees of 1936. It appeared certain that the Giants would far exceed these totals, and the fans packed the Polo Grounds game after game to watch Ott's "windowbreakers," as club secretary Eddie Brannick affectionately referred to them. As early as July 20, the club drew its one millionth customer, an unheard-of attendance at the old park under Coogan's Bluff.

The Giants slipped to fourth place in August. Through it all Ott displayed a new serenity. One writer theorized, "Mel has built a terrific offense in his own image. If the club can trade some of that surplus power for some pitching help during the offseason, the Giants will be something to reckon with in 1948. Mel feels that way and that's why he's calmed down."

Arthur Daley wrote about Ott's empathy for his players:

> During his first few years as manager Ott for a time tried to play out of character. Self-conscious of . . . the reputation of being a shy, retiring sort of bloke . . . he got pretty tough with . . . umpires as well as his own players.
>
> But that has long since worn off. Back to his natural self he works quietly, makes the best moves as he sees them and lets it go at that. If he makes a mistake he accepts the blame. If the player slips up he accepts it as another tough break, providing, of course, the player tried his best.

Ott's feeling for his players was matched by their fondness for him. This personal liking for the manager (criticized by some of Ott's detractors as "friendly disrespect") was reflected in the practical jokes the players pulled on him. Bob Broeg, in a 1976 column in *The Sporting News* on Walker Cooper, told of an incident recounted by Buddy Blattner:

> What he (Cooper) did . . . when we were playing for Ottie was so funny it was almost obscene. . . . Time and again, with Ottie deep in thought. (Cooper) would slip a lighted cigarette in the boss' hip pocket, seconds before Ottie would reach into his pocket to draw out his lineup card. So one day Ott pulled out his pockets, but Cooper was ahead of him. He'd snipped off the pocket linings. So when Ott stuck the batting order cards in his hip pocket, oops! . . . Blattner imitated an embarrassed Ott standing at the plate before 40,000 at the Polo Grounds, trying to fish down the inside of his uniform pants for the lineup cards.

From mid-August on, all hopes of contending for the pennant ended as the Dodgers and Cards pulled further ahead of the Giants. Nevertheless, the fans continued to pour into the Polo Grounds, and the 1946 home attendance record was broken on August 22. Home runs kept exploding off Giant bats, and the Cubs' old National League record was surpassed on August 24. The Yanks' record was broken on September 1 on a homer by Lucky Lohrke, who was not one of the Giant big guns.

The combination of the Giants' explosive hitting and the Dodgers' struggle for the pennant brought out a series of tremendous crowds in a four-game set at the Polo Grounds in early September. Although the Giants were mired in fourth place, 14 games behind the league-leading Dodgers, more than 166,000 rabid fans poured into the old horseshoe-shaped ball park in four days. Vic Lombardi shut the Giants out in the first game before almost 50,000 on a Thursday afternoon. The next day Larry Jansen, who had pitched 10 straight complete game wins, was knocked out of the box in a tense, nip-and-tuck loss before a large crowd. On Saturday, before 43,000 roaring fans, Ray Poat, a righthander just acquired from Baltimore, beat the Dodgers' Ralph Branca on a two-out, last-of-the-ninth homer by Walker Cooper.

On Sunday the crowd started to queue up at the gates at six in the morning. By the time the gates opened at 11 o'clock the line extended all the way out to Old Manhattan Field, the large, vacant field outside the ball park behind the first base and right field stands. Koslo started against Clyde King before more than 51,000 frenzied fans. The Giants went off to a three-run lead in the first inning when Marshall clubbed his 35th home run. Kerr drove in three more runs with a fourth inning homer. "Big Jawn" Mize, his round, red face bulging with an oversized chew of tobacco, rammed his 46th four-master into the upper right field stands in the bottom of the seventh to put the Giants ahead, 7 to 2. But the determined Dodgers clawed their way back with four runs on homers by Cookie Lavagetto and Gene Hermanski to drive Koslo, Andy Hansen, and Jansen to cover and cut the Giant lead to 7 to 6 with only one out in the eighth inning. In desperation, Ott brought in Ken Trinkle, the last pitcher left in whom the little manager had any confidence in a spot like this. With the fans roaring on every pitch, Trinkle outdid himself. He rubbed out Stanky and Reese to end the inning, then erased Reiser, Bruce Edwards, and Dixie Walker in the ninth to win the game.

Playing no favorites, the Giants knocked the second place Cardinals out of the race the next week in St. Louis by sweeping a three-game set in characteristic style. Jansen won his 19th game, beating Jim Hearn easily behind homers by Cooper and Thomson. Trinkle beat Alpha Brazle in relief in the second game, 10 to 5, as Cooper supported him with another home run. In the final game Ray Poat outpitched Harry Brecheen as Gordon and Cooper backed him with circuit clouts. Big Coop carried it off with a flourish, finishing off his old club with a booming, 450-foot drive that seemed to have lost little velocity as it crashed into the bleachers in dead center field.

Ott's club moved on to Chicago, and with nothing at stake, he started two rookies just up from Minneapolis. One was Bobby Rhawn, a second baseman who would have a short, uneventful major league career. The other youngster, catcher Wes Westrum, spent 10 years as a player with the Giants and then managed the club after its move to San Francisco. That same day Whitey Lockman, starting to work his healing leg back into shape, broke into his first game of the campaign.

The Giants returned home and finished their home season on September 21 as Jansen won his 20th game. The club ran off a record-breaking string of 18 consecutive games with at least one home run, and the fans continued to respond as home attendance soared to 1,599,784, almost 380,000 more than the 1946 record.

On September 20, Ott announced his retirement as a player after 22 years with the club. Mel had made only four, unsuccessful pinch-hitting appearances during the season. His last turn at bat came against the Pirates on June 11 when he batted for Trinkle and popped to short. The Giant manager had to appreciate the glowing stories about him in the New York newspapers over the next few days although he reacted with typical self-deprecation. Ott told Arthur Daley, who had written a particularly laudatory column about him, "Thanks for the kind words. I mailed your column home to my wife and I told her this was my obituary notice and I hoped she liked it."

The Polo Grounders wound up the season in fourth place, 13 games behind the pennant-winning Dodgers and five games in back of the third place Braves. Ott's "windowbreakers" hit 221 home runs, 39 more than the 1936 Yankees' old record. The new record stood until the Cincinnati Reds tied it in 1956 when the league home run total was much higher, indicative of a livelier ball. Then, with a longer schedule of 162 games, the Yankees hit 240 homers in 1961.

Individually, the 1947 Giants were not a colorful group. There was no team pixie like Danny Gardella, no battling gamecock like Dick Bartell. It was essentially a team of strong, silent men who did their talking with their bats. Still, they were fun to watch, and some of their individual performances were outstanding.

Mize tied the Pirates' Ralph Kiner for the home run lead with 51, and Marshall, Cooper, and Thomson ranked third, fourth, and fifth. Mize led in RBI's, and Cooper and Marshall were in the top five. The three sluggers also were in the top five in total bases, and Mize led the circuit in runs scored. Jansen, with a sparkling 21 and 5 record, led the league in winning percentage and was in the top five in wins and complete games. Koslo won 15 and lost 10, and Trinkle led in games pitched and was third in saves. And Kerr led all the shortstops in assists. Despite these excellent performances, many dismissed the team as "sluggish" and "uninspired." The simple truth is that the club would probably have won the pennant easily with only a reasonably competent pitching staff.

Stoneham and Ott, looking forward to better things in 1948, went to another subway series between the Yanks and Dodgers. They saw the Bronx Bombers win a great seven-game set. It featured Yankee Bill Bevens' one-hit game loss to the Dodgers on Cookie Lavagetto's two-out-in-the-ninth double and Al Gionfriddo's famous catch of Joe DiMaggio's long drive in front of the visitor's bullpen at Yankee Stadium. Many fans watched the World Series on small, seven-inch TV sets, then coming into wide use.

During the Series, it was announced that Danny Gardella had sued the Giants, the Commissioner, the major league presidents, and the head of the minor leagues for $300,000, charging that the reserve clause "is monopolistic and tends to restrain trade and commerce." Gardella's claim (which was dismissed a year later) was nothing new then, and the issue remained unresolved until almost 30 years later.

15

Exit Ott — Enter Durocher

Over the winter it was the same old story—plenty of talk about trading for established players, but nothing came of it. And very few writers and fans shared Ott's professed optimism that the pitching would somehow improve.

Jansen, coming off a great rookie year, was expected to be the staff ace. Ken Trinkle was a solid reliever, but there were no other heavyweights on the staff. Koslo had undergone elbow surgery. Ray Poat, Andy Hansen, and Sheldon Jones had not proven themselves. Hartung had been erratic. Monty Kennedy was still wild and inconsistent. Joe Beggs, also back after arm surgery, had been of little use since coming over from the Reds. Bill Ayers and Hub Andrews were back for another try, but Mort Cooper had retired. Then, there were a number of anonymous pitchers up from the farm clubs—unknowns like Red Hardy, Stan Halstead, Lou Lombardo, Mario Picone, and George Spencer.

As spring training moved along the Giants began to collect veteran pitchers who had been cast adrift by other teams. They signed 41-year-old lefthander Thornton Lee, released by the White Sox after 15 years in the American League. Southpaw Vern Olsen, an ex-Cub, had not pitched a major league inning in 1947, but he was trying out with the Giants. Then Ott picked up the well-traveled, 39-year-old Bobo Newsom. Since 1929, Bobo had pitched for eight big league clubs, including several tours of duty with the Senators.

There was another category of Giant pitcher—anyone with a strong arm. In this case it was catcher Jim Gladd, who had caught in four games with the Giants in 1946. Gladd was a weak hitter but his rifle arm attracted the attention of Ott and his coaches. He was given a trial as a pitcher for a couple of weeks, just long enough for him to develop a bad sore arm which ended the experiment abruptly. Over all, the pitching situation

131

seemed hopeless and Ott knew it, although characteristically he was never heard to complain publicly about the lack of help provided him by the front office.

The rest of the team was pretty well set. Mize was a fixture at first, and Rigney played second with increased assurance. Kerr, after a determined holdout, was at shortstop, and Lohrke appeared to have the inside track at third although he had yet to prove that he could cope with major league pitching. Other infielders in camp included Mickey Witek, Buddy Blattner, Bobby Rhawn, Jack Conway from the Indians, and ex-Cub Lou Stringer. Johnny McCarthy, who had been selected as Bill Terry's successor at first base 12 years before, had been brought up from Minneapolis.

The regular outfield was expected to include Marshall in right with Thomson, Lockman, and Gordon competing strongly for the other two outfield slots. Don Mueller, Joe Lafata, Lloyd Gearhart, and Les Layton, up from Minneapolis, were the other outfielders in camp. Walker Cooper, of course, was the regular catcher. Wes Westrum, Mickey Livingston, Ben Warren, and "good throw-no hit" Jim Gladd were the other catching hopefuls.

The new Giant pitchers showed little as the club barnstormed east with the Indians, and it was clear that Ott would have to rely on his veterans. As the campaign opened, the Associated Press polls projected a fourth-place finish for the Giants, behind the Cards, Braves, and Dodgers.

Leo Durocher had been reinstated and was managing the Dodgers as the Giants opened the season against them before more than 48,000 at the Polo Grounds. It was a bad day all around for the Giants. Buddy Kerr, hit on the head by an outfield throw in one of the final exhibition games, did not play. His loss proved to be crucial as Whitey Lockman collided with Bobby Rhawn, Kerr's inexperienced replacement, permitting a blooper to fall safely and drive in the winning run in a Giant loss. The next day Ott suspended Kerr for refusing to play despite doctors' reports that he was in shape to play. Ott was criticized for the implied charge that Kerr was malingering. But all was forgiven a few days later when Buddy returned to the lineup and flashed his old form.

The Giants were in second place after completing their first series with the eastern clubs. The big surprise was the impeccable pitching of Jones and Poat which matched first-rate outings by Jansen. But even with the pitchers doing better than expected and the offense coming along, the Giants had a serious problem. Walker Cooper had sustained a chipped bone in his knee in the first week of the season, and the big fellow underwent surgery that was expected to sideline him for two months.

The club played slip-shod ball on its first western trip as the pitching and hitting slipped. To make matters worse, the Giants were guilty of a number of errors that cost ball games. Typical was a game in Chicago when they blew a 6 to 0 lead to lose 8 to 7 on a succession of mechanical and mental errors. The Cub's winning run scored on an incredible lapse by Trinkle. With the game tied, two out in the bottom of the ninth, and Cub runners on second and third, Trinkle got Peanuts Lowrey to hit an easy bounder back to the box. Instead of throwing to first for the routine third out, Trinkle threw to the plate thinking there was only one out. The throw to an amazed Mickey Livingston was too late, almost skulling the surprised catcher, as Eddie Waitkus scored the winning run. After the game, Ott gave his blundering charges a blistering that would have done credit to John McGraw.

The Giants did poorly on their next home stand and slipped down to fourth place, four games out of first. The club struggled through to the All-Star game break, eight games out of the lead with a 36 and 37 record. Cooper returned to the lineup, but even having the big Missourian back did not help the pitching which reached a new low. Twice in a week Ott called upon seven pitchers in futile attempts to win games.

Early on the morning of July 16, a bombshell burst. Bill Corum, in an exclusive story in the *Journal-American*, reported that Ott had been fired, Durocher had been named to replace him, and Burt Shotton again had been called out of semi-retirement to take over the Dodgers. Beginning with the Giants' unimpressive play in June there had been a resurgence of the old rumors that Ott was on the way out, but they were not taken seriously. With the Dodgers floundering after their pennant win in 1947, there also had been rumors of Durocher's dismissal, but here too little credence was placed in the stories. Even then, if either manager had been let out in unrelated moves, this would have been accepted as part of the game. But Durocher the new boss at the Polo Grounds! To Giant fans this was unthinkable. As Ken Smith wrote in the *Daily Mirror*, ''Giant fans hated Durocher because he was a Dodger. To drop him suddenly in the Polo Grounds, where the feats of McGraw, Terry, Ott, Matty, and the others are a sacred memory, was a shock too abrupt for acceptance.''

The Giants held a news conference at the club offices later in the morning with Stoneham, Durocher, Ott, Hubbell, and publicity director Garry Schumacher on hand. The questions flew thick and fast as reporters tried to piece together the sequence of events.

When had Stoneham decided to make the change? At about one o'clock the day before. It was shortly before the double-header with the Pirates. Ott, of course, was with the club. Durocher was in Montreal looking over Dodger farm talent.

Was the change a surprise to Ott? Stoneham told writers, ''I had already discussed this with Ottie. He was the one who suggested getting Durocher if it were possible.''

What about getting the okay to talk to Durocher? Stoneham responded, ''I called Ford Frick and obtained his approval. I then contacted Rickey and told him we would like to have Leo manage the Giants. I was agreeably surprised when Rickey gave me permission to negotiate with Leo. I met with Leo about 10:30 last night at his apartment and we came to terms pretty quickly."

What was Durocher's reaction? The Lippy One started off like a diplomat. "I feel the change will do me a lot of good because I have always like Ott and Stoneham and their organization. Of course," he added quickly, "I also was very happy in Brooklyn and I definitely was never asked to resign." (In a story from Pittsburgh datelined July 17, the next day, the United Press quoted Durocher as saying that on July 4, Dodger press secretary Harold Parrott had told him, "The boss wants you to resign, Leo." Durocher told Parrott that he ". . . wouldn't resign. They'd have to fire me.")

What changes would he make in the Giants? Durocher looked at the writers, their pens poised as if to impale him, and he turned uncharacteristically reticent. "I have nothing to say on that one. I have some ideas, but I want to talk them over with Mel before I make any changes."

A few more questions and the press conference was over. Durocher, Stoneham, Hubbell, and Garry Schumacher left immediately for Pittsburgh to join the team. And Ott, after a few quiet goodbys, somberly walked out of the Giant offices and disappeared in the crowd on 42nd Street. The next day the Giants permanently retired his Number 4 uniform. After almost 23 years, that was the last field job Ott would have with the Giants although he took on a variety of tasks with Hubbell until his contract expired in 1950.

James P. Dawson of the *New York Times* wrote of the players' reaction to the change in leadership:

> The end of Master Melvin's reign, although not unexpected, nevertheless came with bombshell-like effect on the squad. The engagement of Durocher aggravated the shock. The change finds the Giants playing under orders of a leader on whom they have been riding hard since his return from last year's exile.
>
> For obvious reasons none of the players would openly discuss the change. One of them summed up the situation as follows: "Ball players are supposed to play ball to the best of their ability, not concern themselves with the operations of the front office."
>
> That they regretted the passing of Ott was plain, particularly the startling manner in which the Ott reign ended. It was generally held the change was influenced by the front office, that something had to be done and, as is generally the case in such circumstances, Ott became the sacrificial goat.

Most Giant fans fumed about having Durocher at the Polo Grounds, although there were some who thought it was a stroke of genius on Stoneham's part. Still, it was hard to find a Giant fan who was not saddened by Ott's departure. In today's sports world, where fans are more blasé, managerial changes rarely cause much excitement. But in 1948,

New York was a city that took its baseball and its emotional involvement with long-standing heroes like Ott very seriously. Fans gathered everywhere—offices, bars, restaurants, streets—and discussed the change.

Some Giant rooters were against the change unequivocally. "Hell, they should have got Mel some pitchers. That's all he needed," said one. A fashionable Park Avenue matron snapped, "From now on, I'm an ex-Giant fan." George Chefalo of Peekskill, New York, a leading Giant rooter for nearly 25 years, said emphatically, "That settles it, brother. I'm through. I'll never go to the Polo Grounds again." He was asked, "What if Durocher leads them to a pennant?" Chefalo rejected that idea out of hand with a curt, "That's impossible."

Other Giant fans saw it differently. One rejoiced, "It means the pennant. With that power, Durocher will blow the league apart." Another commented, "We couldn't beat the Dodgers under Ott so we had to get a manager who can. Personally, I don't care for Durocher but we had to make a change."

Durocher was out of favor with most Dodger fans. One said, "I never wished the Giants anything but bad luck, but I didn't think they'd get it wrapped up in one neat package." Another Dodger rooter related the change to his finances with the comment, "It's like taking a pay cut. I haven't spent a dime in Ebbets Field this year. But with Durocher gone, I'll be buying four or five tickets again." Another Brooklynite analyzed the change in terms of the Dodgers' finances. "That Rickey is a smart guy. He gets rid of Durocher who's liked by less than half of the people and who gets a big salary, and he brings back a guy that everyone likes who gets a much lower salary."

There were a couple of interesting details on the managerial upheaval that came out later. One had to do with Stoneham's strategy in obtaining Rickey's agreement to release Durocher. After Ott recommended Durocher as his successor, Stoneham had wondered how best to gain Leo's release. Stoneham felt that the Dodgers would be glad to see Durocher go, but the Giant owner was afraid that Rickey would turn down a direct request for the Giants to approach Leo. So Stoneham attacked the matter more indirectly.

The late, long-time Giant broadcaster Russ Hodges described Stoneham's approach in Hodges' book, *My Giants*. According to Hodges, Stoneham's chance came as he flew to St. Louis for the All-Star game two weeks before Ott's ouster. On the plane Stoneham met Frank Shaughnessy, the president of the International League and a close friend of Rickey's.

"Frank," said Stoneham, "do you think Burt Shotton might be available to manage the Giants?"

"I don't know," Shaughnessy answered, "but I can ask Rickey. Do you want me to sound him out?"

Stoneham told Shaughnessy to go ahead. A few days later Shaughnessy brought back word that Shotton wasn't available, but would Durocher do instead? Stoneham said that Leo would do very nicely indeed and that paved the way for Leo's availability. If Hodges' account is accurate, it contradicts Stoneham's press conference response that he was "agreeably surprised" on July 15, the day he said that Rickey informed him that Durocher was available.

Then there was the matter of Bill Corum's exclusive story. Rickey and Stoneham had agreed to release the story simultaneously on July 16 in New York and in Pittsburgh. Rickey was enraged when Corum's scoop appeared in advance of the agreed-upon announcement time. Although both the Giants and the Dodgers had taken precautions to guard against a news leak, Garry Schumacher, who knew Durocher well, was positive that the story would come out prematurely. According to Russ Hodges' account, Schumacher deliberately spent the night of July 15 with Stoneham to make sure that he (Schumacher) wouldn't be held responsible for any leak. Just as Schumacher anticipated, Durocher called Corum as soon as the deal was set with Stoneham to ask Corum what he thought of it. Presumably, Corum expressed his opinion and then immediately filed the story. The net result—a big scoop for Corum and, more importantly, a new manager at the Polo Grounds.

16

"The Giants Is Dead"

When Ott was deposed, the Giants were in a fourth-place tie with the Dodgers, 8½ games behind the first-place Braves and playing at a .493 clip. The club spurted briefly in the first few games under Durocher but then fell back, burdened by its inescapable pitching shortcomings. The team played at a .519 pace under Durocher and finished in fifth place as the Braves held on to win the pennant. In effect, Durocher did no better with the team than Ott. As the season ended, one of my fellow fans in the bleachers commented, "Maybe nice guys and not-so-nice guys finish in pretty much the same place—just as far as their talent takes them."

None of my bleacher buddies had any particular regard for Durocher, and some of them disliked him intensely. Yet, even with the club doing no better and with a manager no one liked, we continued to congregate in the right field bleacher seats. After all, baseball was still our game and the Giants were still our team. And it was pleasant sitting there hours before the game with old friends—talking baseball, watching the players practice, and listening to the shouts of the players, vendors, and fans and the crack of the batted balls echoing around the nearly empty old ball park.

Louie was still the king of the bleachers. His only noticeable changes since the 1930's were a bigger paunch and greyer sideburns. But, most important, his enthusiasm for the game and his rapport with the players were undiminished.

We talked a lot about the men who had played during the Terry and Ott years. Travis Jackson and that rifle arm. Blondy Ryan and his unshakeable confidence despite his limited ability. Hank Leiber and all that potential that went up in smoke after Feller beaned him. Tarzan Parmelee and all that stuff competing with his wildness. The canny, bottle-shaped Dolph Luque. Hal Schumacher and his arm-wrenching delivery and bulldog determination. Fat Freddy Fitzsimmons pitching as if he were on a turntable. That gazelle Whitehead. Bantamweight Dick Bartell, who would smile like an angel just before getting into a fight with someone twice his size. Jo-Jo Moore, and how could such a thin, weak-looking man hit and throw such line drives and play that left field wall so perfectly? Plodding and dependable Gus Mancuso. Billy Jurges, always wrestling with Ott and playing shortstop so effortlessly when his aching head permitted. Buddy Kerr—the poor man's Slats Marion. Happy-go-lucky Harry Danning, and what's a nice Jewish boy doing with a batting stance like Rogers Hornsby? Sam Leslie who could hit if you woke him up at two in the morning but who couldn't field when you played him at two in the afternoon. Cliff Melton and that toothy grin like a character out of Steinbeck's *Of Mice and Men*. The relaxed Babe Young. Unpredictable Danny Gardella and Bill Voiselle who got untracked for only one year. And the strong, silent window-breakers of 1947—Mize, Cooper, Marshall, Gordon, and the rest. But most of the talk was of Hubbell, Ott, and Terry—the three greatest Giants of those years.

The young bleacher bugs loved to hear Louie talk about the players because of his voluminous knowledge and his vivid descriptions, but mostly for his sophisticated analyses of the players and their styles. One day one of the younger fans asked Louie what Hubbell was like. It was like winding up a clock. Louie said:

"When most people talk about Hubbell they usually have in mind his screwball, his 18-inning masterpiece against the Cards in 1933, his 1934 All-Star game strikeout feat, that kind of stuff. I don't think of his individual games. I think of an artist painting a portrait, every stroke of the brush with a purpose. Or a chessmaster who studies every move with the same detached concentration whether he's playing or just watching. Hub would start a batter off with a curve and it was usually a beaut, always low and on the corner of the plate. Then, with that uncanny control and that good speed of his, he'd bust one in, either on the fists or high and outside. Then maybe a changeup. Next, the screwball. Jeez, what a pitch! It gave those righthand hitters fits, especially after Hub set them up with the curve and the fast ball."

Louie's eyes sparkled as he thought of the lanky Oklahoman with the number 11 uniform and with the trouser legs bloused well below his knees. He continued, "Hub was great in the clutch. He won for years with a low-scoring team and he won the big games consistently. Also, he won more than he lost against the great pitchers of his time—Dizzy Dean, Lon Warneke, Paul Derringer and the other great ones. His only weakness was that the Dodgers were his jinx team and that was rough, the Giant-Dodger rivalry being what it is."

He went on, "Hubbell had the perfect temperament. He never got excited or lost his concentration when we blew an easy chance behind him. And I used to get a kick just watching him in the dugout on days he wasn't pitching. Even at the end of his career when he'd seen it all, he would sit there quietly and never take his eyes off the batter or the pitcher. I think he knew their strengths and weaknesses better than they did themselves. All in all, Hub was the greatest lefthander I've ever seen and most of the players I know feel the same." (Hubbell, voted into the Hall of Fame in 1947, remained in charge of player personnel for the San Francisco club until the Stoneham group sold the Giants in 1976.)

Another time one of the older fans was talking about Ott. He said, "Let's face it, Mel was just too nice a guy to be a manager. He felt he had to act tough because he thought the players and the umpires would try to take advantage of him. But he couldn't stay that way long and I think some of the fellows did take advantage. I never thought he could handle pitchers either."

A second fan didn't see it that way. He commented, "I don't agree. I don't think Mel was the ideal manager type either, but he never had any pitching. How many real pitchers did he ever have? Cliff Melton wasn't much by the time Ott took over. Voiselle had one good year, but even after we traded him he didn't win. Koslo is a willing, steady-type pitcher, and Ace Adams was great before he jumped to Mexico. But other than Larry Jansen, Mel never really had a pitching ace. Heck, the front office didn't help him and he tried everything, a coach (Kress), a catcher who could throw bullets (Gladd), and all those washed-up guys like Lee and Newsom. No, Ottie never had a chance."

Louie tired of the discussion and cut in. "I don't like to think about Mel as a manager," he said. "He didn't have the temperament, the ruthlessness, the front office support, or the luck. But as a player, that's something else!"

We all listened as the perceptive Louie continued. "Talk about Ott as a player and what do most people think about? The unorthodox batting style, the short right field wall and all those home runs. How young he was when he started, what a natural he was, and how small he was to be such a big hitter. But to me, that's not the real story of Ott." Louie paused and went on. "I think Mel Ott was one of the most underrated of the great players I've seen. For one thing, he's so quiet and unassuming that he never got the publicity he deserved even though he played in New York. He wasn't flashy and he played almost every game every year no matter how he felt with those charleyhorses and other injuries. He was just a solid little guy with an uncanny ability to make the big play at bat or in the field more consistently than any player I've ever seen. He was a great clutch hitter, particularly in the late innings, and I mean all kinds of hits, not just homers. They don't keep records on game-winning hits (they do today), but I'm sure Mel would rank near the top if they did."

Louie was just getting warmed up talking about his favorite player. "There's so much more to say about Ottie. He was so versatile and unselfish that he would play anywhere. I've always thought we won the pennant in 1937 only because he volunteered to play third so we could get Jimmy Ripple's bat in the lineup. Remember, the Giants were a weak-hitting team for so many years and that put a big strain on Ott because they could pitch around him. Don't forget that Terry batted ahead of Mel, not after him. Besides Hank Leiber in 1935 and Johnny Mize in 1942, Ottie didn't hit in front of a big hitter like all of the home run hitters I can think of—Ruth before Gehrig, Gehrig ahead of DiMaggio or Dickey, Foxx before Cronin, just for a few examples. That's why Mel got so many walks.

"There were other things I remember. Ott could hit to left field when it was necessary, McGraw made sure he learned that when he was a kid. And, for a home run hitter, he was an excellent bunter and Terry often had him sacrifice. Another thing people don't realize was that very few of the other sluggers struck out as infrequently as Ott in relation to the number of walks he drew. That's important because nothing kills a rally as fast as a strikeout. You don't advance runners when you don't hit the ball.

"Then, of course, Mel was the best right fielder in the game for a long time; judging flies, playing the wall, throwing, and keeping the runners close to the bases. He was no speedboy. But, even then, he was a smart, tough base-runner and he hit into very few double plays because they played him for a sharp pull hitter—way to the right side and deep. No, great as he was, I don't think Ott was fully appreciated except by the guys who played with him or against him and by people who watched him closely year after year. On top of that, he was a sweet guy. Just a wonder-ful, unspoiled kid when he came up and he never changed." (Ott, who was voted into the Hall of Fame in 1951, died tragically at 49 after an automobile accident.)

"How about Terry?" one of the younger fans asked. Louie responded, "Terry was a different kind of guy. He was a mature man with a family when McGraw brought him up and he was never awed by the big city like Hubbell and Ott were for a time. To Terry, the money was right and the Giants were just another big league team. I always thought his attitude was strictly what's in it for me.

"Terry was a great player, though. He was a smart, line drive hitter, and he didn't try to pull the ball unless the situation demanded it. He always hit for a high average because he scattered those line shots so well. His .401 average in 1930 was no fluke. Terry had lots of guts, too. I'll never forget the way he forced himself to play in 1936 when his knees were in such bad shape. And he was the best first baseman I ever saw. He was a big guy but he covered a lot of ground and no one could make that first-to-second-to-first double play any better. The man was really grace-ful around the bag. A lot of the oldtimers thought he was better than George Sisler, and that's saying a lot."

One of the older fans interjected, "He was a good manager, too." Louie said, "Terry was a hell of a manager. I heard that some of his players didn't care for him. They thought he didn't care about their problems and he could be a tough guy to deal with at contract time. Some of the players who didn't go back to the old McGraw days thought that Terry was a cold fish. And he wasn't a colorful guy, although I always thought he provoked the Dodgers on purpose just to build up the gate receipts. Another rap was that he won only as long as the players McGraw left him were still around—Hubbell, Ott, Fitzsimmons, Jackson, and Terry himself. That's true up to a point. After all, he won three pennants before those guys wore out and none after 1937 when Ott was the only fellow with much left. But, don't forget, Terry made those pennants possible with three big trades. Getting Mancuso won the 1933 pennant, and the Bartell and Whitehead deals brought us the pennants in 1936 and 1937.

"Terry was one of the best field strategists I've ever seen. In 1933 he brought back the old idea of playing for one run early in the game, and it really worked. He knew how to handle his pitchers. And his teams were drilled in the fundamentals—the cutoff play, throwing to the right base, bunting, sliding, and general heads-up play. He got the most out of his players or they didn't last long with the Giants.

"His personal relations with the writers were lousy, though. He alienated them by playing hard to get, and he made it worse by discouraging his players from talking to reporters. He got away with it while the team was winning, but he got a terrible press when we stopped winning. And the fans never warmed to the guy. Some thought he was out for all he could get and to hell with everything else."

Still, several of Terry's players spoke well of their old boss in conversations with the writer. For example, I had a long talk with Cliff Melton in January 1978, during which he had nothing but praise for Memphis Bill. "Old Bill was a mighty nice man to play for and was always fair with me," Melton told me in his deep Carolina drawl. "We were always a close group and Terry would go out and drink beer with us. He respected our opinions on baseball matters, and he would even ask us in clubhouse meetings before big games who we would prefer to have pitch the game. I got my biggest thrill when the fellers asked Bill to let me pitch a clutch game against the Cubs in 1937 and I was able to win it. Terry also was very helpful to me on business matters. Once I was offered $100 to endorse a product. When I mentioned it to Bill he asked me if I had signed anything yet. I said no. So Bill got in the act, and I wound up getting $2,500 through his efforts. I always thought the world of him."

Apparently Terry mellowed with the passing years. There was an interesting story that came out of the Hall of Fame installation ceremonies at Cooperstown in 1974. Mickey Mantle gave a lighthearted acceptance speech. Then he amazed everyone by concluding that he ". . . hoped to live up to Bill Terry's expectations." St. Louis sportswriter Bob Broeg explained the background behind Mantle's reference to the supposedly callous Terry. Broeg recounted that the night before the installation ceremonies Terry urged Mantle and his fellow inductee, Whitey Ford, to plan to visit Cooperstown each summer when new members are installed because all Hall of Fame members "owed it to the game."

Broeg recalled that Terry, miffed over having to wait until 1954 to be voted to the Hall of Fame, had replied icily, "I have nothing to say," when informed of his election. But the crusty guy from Memphis thawed out after his belated selection. As Broeg wrote in *The Sporting News* in September 1974, "He (Terry) has become a faithful figure at Hall of Fame functions and, quietly, a champion of those financially needy. At 76, a wealthy Jacksonville automobile dealer, Terry could sit down there in Florida and clip coupons, but he believes that even though he felt baseball owed him every penny he earned as a tough bargainer at the salary negotiating table as well as home plate, he owes baseball something—his time and attention."

* * * * *

Giant fans came back in 1949 to see how Durocher would do in his first full year managing the club. But 1949 was a repeat of 1948 as the club finished in fifth place again. Mize and Cooper slumped badly, and only Bobby Thomson and Sid Gordon had good years. Lippy Leo was exasperated by the Giants' failure, and he was pressured further by a strong Dodger showing that led to another pennant. He proclaimed during the late summer that he was going to build "my kind of team," one built on speed and aggressiveness rather than power.

Durocher began to clean house long before the season ended. Cooper, having a poor year and never a Durocher admirer, was traded to the Reds for catcher Ray Mueller. Mize, hitting .263 with a mere 18 home runs, was sold to the Yankees in time to star in the World Series against the Dodgers. During the winter the Giants made a whopper of a deal that completed the transformation begun with the Cooper trade. Willard Marshall, Sid Gordon, and Buddy Kerr were dealt to the Braves for second baseman Eddie Stanky and shortstop Alvin Dark. Durocher was building his kind of team.

In 1950 the Giants moved up, finishing only five games behind Manager Eddie Sawyer's Whiz Kid Phillies. Robin Roberts, Curt Simmons, and reliever Jim Konstanty supplied the Phil's pitching, and Del Ennis and Willie (Puddinhead) Jones were the big hitters. Still, things were looking up for the Giants. The team had more pep and speed. Stanky and Dark solidified the club around second base. After a so-so year in 1949, Larry Jansen rebounded with 19 wins. And the Giants got a big break as Sal Maglie returned from Mexico a tough, seasoned pitcher who had learned a lot from Dolph Luque. Durocher himself had calmed down to the point where the writers referred to him as "The Little Shepherd of Coogan's Bluff."

1951 was the incredible year of the Bobby Thomson home run—the year of the Miracle of Coogan's Bluff. The Giants' opening lineup included their first two black players, Monte Irvin at first and Hank Thompson at third, both of whom had joined the club in 1949, Stanky, and Dark. Don Mueller, called "Mandrake the Magician" because of his deft bat control, was the right fielder. Thomson was in center with Lockman in left. Wes Westrum was the catcher. The regular starters were Jansen, Maglie, Koslo, George Spencer, and Jim Hearn, who was acquired from the Cardinals in 1950.

The 1951 club started slowly and Durocher made some changes. He switched Lockman and Irvin and replaced Thomson in center with a young fellow just up from Minneapolis where he was hitting a cool .477—the incomparable Willie Mays. After a slow start, Mays began to spark the club with his spirited play and morale-boosting good nature. Yet, on August 11, the Giants were a distant 13½ games behind Charlie Dressen's league-leading Dodgers. Durocher's club bounced back dramatically and cut the lead to five games with a 16-game winning streak, then pulled dead even as the regular season ended.

In the three-game playoff for the pennant, Hearn beat Ralph Branca 3 to 1 in the first game, but the Dodgers squared matters as Clem Labine won 10 to 0. The famous deciding game came the next day at the Polo Grounds as Maglie faced big Don Newcombe. The Dodgers held a 4 to 1 lead going into the bottom of the ninth, and Newcombe seemed to be throwing as hard as he had all day. Dark and Mueller opened with singles, but Irvin popped out. Lockman doubled in Dark and sent Mueller to third. With the Giants behind 4 to 2 and one out, Thomson stepped up.

Dressen waved in Branca from the bullpen, and the ensuing scene is as familiar to today's fans, who have viewed the film so often on television, as to those at the Polo Grounds on that long-ago, early October afternoon. Thomson swung mightily at Branca's second pitch and the ball buzzed on a line into the lower left field stands. Giant announcer Russ Hodges screamed, "The Giants win the pennant, the Giants win the pennant. I don't believe it. Oooh boy, the Giants win the pennant!" Stanky sprinted out of the Giant dugout, headed straight for Durocher who was coaching at third, and ecstatically wrestled the Giant manager to the ground. The Giants greeted Thomson en masse at the plate, while the stunned Branca walked slowly off the mound, barely comprehending that the pennant had been lost by one pitch. The Giants' loss to the Yanks in the World Series was strictly an anticlimax.

The Giants finished in second place in 1952 as the Dodgers came back to win. Irvin missed most of the year with a broken ankle, and Mays was called up by the Army early in the season. Hearn, Maglie, and reliever

Hoyt Wilhelm carried the pitching load as Jansen faltered, but the Giants were outclassed.

1953 was a leaner year with Mays in the service for the entire season, and the Giants fell back to fifth place. Maglie, Jansen, and Hearn had poor years, Wilhelm was less effective, and the only bright spot was provided by rookie pitcher Ruben Gomez, who won 13 games. The Giants were out of the race by midsummer, and Charlie Dressen emphatically counted them out in August with the accurate, if ungrammatical, pronouncement, "The Giants is dead."

1954 provided a pleasant surprise as the Giants came back to win the pennant. The offense was paced by the booming bat of the returned Willie Mays. Lockman, Dark, and Hank Thompson had good seasons, and a colorful Alabaman, Jim (Dusty) Rhodes, had a remarkable year as a pinch hitter, coming through in the clutch time after time. Lefthander Johnnie Antonelli, a former bonus baby obtained from the Braves (then based in Milwaukee), led the pitching staff with a brilliant 21 and 7 record. Gomez, Maglie, Marv Grissom, and Wilhelm were the pitching reliables as the Giants beat out the Dodgers by five games. This was Walter Alston's first year managing the Dodgers, as Dressen and Dodger owner Walter O'Malley were unable to agree on a multiyear contract for Dressen. 1954 proved to be Durocher's biggest year as his team beat a strong Cleveland club in four straight in the World Series. This Series is remembered best for Mays' incredible, over-the-shoulder catch of Vic Wertz' long drive almost to the right center field bleacher screen at the Polo Grounds.

1955 was Durocher's last year as Giant manager as the club slipped back to third place, 18½ games behind another powerful Dodger club. The Giants had three new regulars: first baseman Gail Harris, second baseman Wayne Terwilliger, and catcher Ray Katt. None of them came through, the pitching was mediocre, and another great season by Mays was wasted. Durocher's contract ran out and was not renewed.

Bill Rigney, who had managed at Minneapolis in 1954 and 1955, was picked to succeed Durocher. But the Giants finished sixth as Alston's "Boys of Summer" won again. The peppery Rigney had little to work with. Antonelli had another great year. Otherwise, the pitching staff's weakness reminded the fans of Ott's tribulations years before. Mays, after a slow start, belted 36 home runs, and young Bill White, a rookie first baseman, showed promise. Giant fans were unhappy with the team's performance but concerned most about rumors that the franchise might be moved.

The story was the same in 1957. A sixth-place finish, inept pitching except for Gomez who won 15 games, and a generally mediocre club with weaknesses relieved only by the brilliant play of Mays and the occasional power hitting of Hank Sauer, who had come over from the Cardinals.

In 1955 it had become public knowledge that O'Malley wanted to move the Dodgers out of Ebbets Field with its limited capacity. Plans were announced to play seven games in 1956 in larger, more modern, Roosevelt Stadium in Jersey City. This had been the home field of the Jersey City Giants, who had ceased operations. At the same time that O'Malley was taking steps to move the Dodgers, Stoneham was looking for another home for his team. With the Polo Grounds slated to be demolished and replaced by a housing development, it was rumored that Stoneham was considering renting Yankee Stadium—full cycle from the early 1920's when the Yanks were ousted from the Polo Grounds by John McGraw. But it was clear that the eventual decision as to where to transplant the Giants would depend upon where the Dodgers went.

After long, unproductive negotiations between the Dodgers and Brooklyn borough officials, O'Malley openly expressed his disenchantment with the Brooklyn setup and his interest in moving the team to Los Angeles. At the same time Stoneham told the writers that he had received an attractive offer to relocate the Giants in San Francisco. Finally, in August 1957, with arrangements all but completed to move the Dodgers to Los Angeles, the Giants announced they would move to San Francisco in time for the 1958 season. To Giant fans it was small consolation to know that the historic Giant-Dodger rivalry would continue almost 3,000 miles away.

The Giants played their last game at the Polo Grounds on September 29, 1957 and lost to the Pirates, 9 to 1. Just as Dusty Rhodes grounded out to end the game, most of the 11,606 fans raced out on the field while the players fled for the safety of the clubhouse. The crowd ripped out home plate, the pitching rubber, the bases, the bullpen fixtures—almost anything that wasn't steel, concrete, or otherwise fastened down. Fans gathered in forlorn groups in center field, many shouting unsuccessfully for the players to come out of the clubhouse. Other shouted insults at Stoneham's empty office.

Mrs. John McGraw, a devoted Giant rooter even in the many years since his death, was the last "official" fan to leave the ball park. She lamented tearfully, "I still can't believe it. This would have broken John's heart. New York will never be the same." The other fans just stood there for a while and then trudged sorrowfully out of the Polo Grounds

I remember walking alone toward the familiar bleacher exit, my head down and my hands in my pockets. I turned around to take one last look at the big, green, horseshoe-shaped stands, the brown basepaths, and the velvety green outfield, now strewn with paper and debris. The field was almost obliterated by groups of angry fans. As I approached the exit I spotted Louie a few rows back, leaving after watching his beloved Giants for the last time. I waved good-bye to him, and he waved back gravely. Then, I remember clearly, his round face broke into a warm smile and he boomed in farewell, "Take care of yourself, kid."